In the Spirit
of the Holidays

In the Spirit of the Holidays

Readings to Enrich Every Jewish Holiday

Down-to-earth poems
on the meaning of
traditions, for you to
use at home
or synagogue.

Janet Ruth Falon

Also by
Janet Ruth Falon
The Jewish Journaling Book
(Jewish Lights Publishing 2004)

CONNECT ONLINE
www.janetfalon.com

Several of Janet Ruth Falon's poems have already appeared in
Jewish Currents, New Menorah, The Jewish Writing Project,
and *All the Women Followed Her: A Collection of Writings on
Miriam the Prophet & The Women of Exodus.*

Published by

STICKY EARTH BOOKS
Exton, Pennsylvania
StickyEarth.com

Paperback ISBN 978-0-9986449-1-2
Library of Congress Control Number: 2018957433

Design and composition by Annette Murray

DEDICATION

For Cary and Hope, with love

TABLE OF CONTENTS

Preface

I used to berate myself when I'd sit in synagogue and my mind wandered instead of staying focused on what was going on in the service. It was easy to blame myself for losing concentration, or to blame the service, or the rabbi, or the particular practices of this congregation, for not fully engaging me. But then I realized if I tuned in to where my mind was wandering, it had often meandered somewhere related to the service, or to the customs of the holiday, or to some idiosyncratic experience I'd had during this holiday in previous years. What I was doing, in essence, was making meaning; creative daydreaming was leading me down a path to some point of convergence, some place where, spiritually speaking, I could hang my hat and feel at home. Unbridled daydreaming was for me a form of prayer; there was some instinct in me, coupled with my desire to make my Judaism work, which was encouraging and permitted me to wander until I landed at a junction that felt true and real and relevant.

Once in a while, my daydreaming led to a dead end. So starting about 30 years ago I began to bring to services with me "Seasons of Our Joy," written by Rabbi Arthur Waskow — a key figure in the Jewish Renewal movement and an inspiring teacher and writer — which describes Waskow's take on every holiday's practices, liturgy, history, etc. That book spoke to me like it knew exactly what I needed to hear. And being stubborn and a bit of a rebel, if what was going on at the *bimah* didn't engage or inspire me, I surreptitiously opened the book to the chapter on that holiday to get Waskow's perspective, and to reconnect myself to the holiday. I also kept a notebook and pen in my purse, and wrote down any resulting thoughts or feelings, which became the foundation for many of the poems in this book.

If you've always observed the Jewish holidays you've heard the story or stories that belong with any particular holiday/s, and observed accompanying rituals and customs, for perhaps as many years as you are old. You've gone through the tension and suspense of the binding-of-Isaac story every *Rosh Hashanah*, first hearing it as a child and now, maybe, relating to it as a parent. Countless times you've dipped your finger in wine as you list, along with everyone else at the *seder* table, the increasingly horrific ten plagues. You've experimented with all sorts of *gragers* — noisemakers — over the years, and finally found one that you're certain is sufficiently loud to drown out Haman's name during the *Megillah* reading at *Purim*. Year after year, the cycle of customs, rituals, and stories of the holidays all become part of you, if only intellectually or reflexively, although maybe in formative, fundamental ways.

So after hearing the telling, and re-telling, of these stories for decades, and years of working out my own ways to make the holidays meaningful, in about 1990 I felt ready to record my own reactions to these stories and customs; many, of course, were germinating for years before.

I was then a member of Or Hadash, a Reconstructionist synagogue now in Fort Washington, Pennsylvania which, when I joined, was still "homeless," meeting at the nearby Reconstructionist Rabbinical College. Led by Rabbi Vivian Schirn, the young congregation was figuring out who and what it was, and in that time of experimentation they allowed me to read my poems at various services. Many members were enthusiastic, which thrilled me, and some of my poems became part of a makeshift holiday prayerbook.

My current synagogue, Kol Ami in Elkins Park, Pennsylvania, has been similarly receptive to my writing, and for many years, until he retired, Founding Rabbi Elliot Holin invited me to write an annual *Yom Kippur* poem and read it at services. One year, a member told me that what she most looked forward to at *Yom Kippur* service was my poem (which, she was quick to add, is not to downplay the power of the rest of the service.)

Several of these poems were written while my husband Cary and I were trying to become biological parents. It was a difficult, faith-shaking decade during which time I "got it," deep down, that life isn't fair. I was angry with God, whom I'd childishly imagined was going to look out for me and give me what I thought I deserved. You'll recognize the poems from that era; the sadness, envy, and rage are easy to spot, and I apologize if my then-fury with God offends you. (It all worked out; we adopted our daughter, Hope, and brought her home from China in 2004. And my spiritual life has been salvaged, albeit with a few nicks and dents that give it its one-of-a-kind texture.)

I'm glad that my relationship with Judaism is sufficiently strong — unbreakable, I assume — that I feel empowered to question, grapple with, and play with its concepts and then have the audacity to write it all down. After all, I'm just me — someone who grew up with a lot of *Yiddishkeit* and parents who transitioned from the observant households of their parents to a Jewish lifestyle they'd reinterpreted to fit their beliefs.

But I am also the granddaughter of four immigrants. My maternal grandfather might have been a kinder soul had he been allowed, at another place and time, to become a rabbi — but he had to work in a sweatshop, cutting layers of fabric with oversized, menacing shears (that I own) to support his family. As far as I know, I have no second or third cousins; the bulk of my ancestors didn't make it to America.

I am a woman who lived with Orthodox roommates in college and learned, and learned to respect, that some people tear toilet paper before *Shabbat* to keep from breaking the prohibition against work. By living with them I received a wonderful education, which included much more substantial information than the toilet-paper rule, for which I am grateful. Also, during those years, I smoked a couple of cigars with the then-rabbi at Boston University's Hillel, the network of Jewish student organizations on college campuses.

I am a feminist who defiantly became a bat mitzvah at age 29. To spite my parents — who hadn't insisted I'd done that when

I was 12, while my brother had — I didn't invite them. (I did tell my parents about it several years later, downplaying my earlier vindictiveness, and they were proud.)

Other bits of Jewish me: I knew I might date but would never marry a non-Jewish man, and I didn't; Cary and I have been compatible partners in living a Jewish life. I felt more at home and connected in Krakow, the big city near Rava-Ruskaya — my mother's family's home — than in Jerusalem, traveling to both places with Jewish singles groups. I have always liked living in predominantly Jewish neighborhoods where I like to think the air on Friday nights smells like chicken soup, and I love the lines that form at the neighborhood Kosher bakery for the High Holidays. Over the years I have taken many courses and workshops, and have had many late-night conversations about how to integrate my Jewish life with my secular life, or vice-versa.

All told, I'm a committed Jew who has always tried to find or make meaning from Judaism. I believe that searching for meaning is what meaning is. These poems are how I did — and do — that.

In spirituality,
the searching is the finding
and the pursuit is the achievement.

— Dr. Abraham J. Twerski

Introduction

When you say "I'm Jewish," the verb that powers that sentence is "to be." "To be" is the epitome of passive verbs; it just hangs there, declaring its identity and responding to changes in the wind like a flag, but not doing much more. But when you engage with Judaism, when you examine it and play with it and let it ripen in your spiritual compost heap, you can transform "being Jewish" into an *active* state of being.

For many Jews, however, being Jewish is mostly a passive experience. They were born Jewish and maybe they acknowledge, somehow, some of the holidays and the life-cycle events. But being Jewish isn't a vital part of themselves to which they devote time and energy, different from how they *do* foster their identity as an ace tennis player, for instance, or a vegetable gardener, or a parent.

Perhaps one of the turn-offs is that to many Jews, practicing Judaism seems to be so serious, so somber, a tradition that seems to rest on prohibitions and restrictions, a no-sayer in a world where "yes" rules. But if you're willing to challenge your perspective — if you're willing to look at the glass and see that it's actually half full (of what is probably Manischewitz concord grape wine from last Passover) — "being Jewish" in the active sense can be stimulating, broadening, and joyful; "I am" is transformed into "I do."

We all know there are many things that turn away today's high-tech, stressed out, tuned-in, information-overloaded people from Judaism (with similar or parallel problems in other religions, too). Traditions are seen as incompatible with today's lifestyles; after all, how can you manage to go to synagogue on Saturday morning when that's your only time to go to the farmers market, plus you have to take one child to a soccer game and another to baseball, and you're committed to catching up on episodes of TV shows you miss during the workweek.

Sexism, too, has been a problem in Judaism (although, happily, it's unraveling, stitch by tightly knit stitch, thanks to a lot of dedicated souls doing vigilant work.) Also troublesome is that many synagogues are still using older prayer books with "thou hast" and "thou art," which makes prayer as inaccessible and seemingly irrelevant as Shakespeare.

Some people point to what they see as hypocrisy: Why should they keep kosher in a world where products like "Bac'n Pieces Bacon-Flavored Bits" allow them to simulate the experience of eating bacon? Or maybe the turn-off is as idiosyncratic as that a synagogue choir's arrangements sound too High Episcopal, or the synagogue building is usually too hot on High Holidays because the air conditioning system has already been shut down for the season.

But the spirit of Judaism and its holidays seems to survive, in some shape, in spite of all sorts of assaults that gnaw at it or blatantly attempt to gouge out chunks; there's something about it that persists, both in people who don't actively practice it as well as in those people who formally abandon it in the most dramatic ways. Even Paul Dubner, who'd converted to Catholicism, sang "My Yiddishe Mama" to his wife, reports his son, Stephen, in his book *Turbulent Souls: A Catholic Son's Return to His Jewish Family.* Even David Gordon, a Jew who not only converts but becomes a rabid anti-Semite (and writer of pious Catholic poetry), blesses his daughter, Mary, every night — in Hebrew — she tells us in *The Shadow Man: A Daughter's Search for Her Father.* Like a tune that sticks with you in spite of your deepest desire to get rid of it — just as "It's a Small World" persists for weeks after a Disneyworld trip — there's something unshakable and tenacious about Judaism and its holidays that burrows in and holds on for dear life.

That connection to Judaism may be as tenuous and wispy as a melody: The dark pleading of "Avenu Malkeynu" at the High Holidays, or the hop-and-skip of Hanukkah's "The Dreidl Song"

("...I made it out of clay...") or the final four-note arc of "ya" in Passover's "Chad Gadya" — or even just a sound, such as the hollow, up-from-the-gut wail of the shofar. In other cases, some people feel connected to the Jewish holidays through a ritual object: *Sukkot's* wonderfully nipply etrog, for instance, wrapped like precious cargo in what looks like a hunk of Rapunzel's golden locks, or an ancestor's menorah encrusted with caked-on wax — or perhaps just a memory, of a *Purim* grogger made in childhood by stapling together two aluminum pie plates filled with dried beans.

Other things that call forth the spirit of Jewish holidays and connect us to them might be food, such as the sweet runniness of home-made cheese blintzes at Shavuot; or the cyclical *bubbe mysers*, such as how your *bubbe* in Brooklyn used to bring home a live carp and let it swim in the bathtub until she was ready to do it in — and then do it up, as gefilte fish — for the holidays; or even a tactile memory, such as the surprising weight and cumbersomeness of the Torah when you first held it, and awkwardly danced with it, at Simhat Torah.

Although we haven't all had the same experience with these particular triggers, it's these types of triggers that unite us. All of us can identify bits or essences of certain holidays — the objects, the tastes and smells and sounds, the stories, the practices, the family traditions, whatever — that have the power to connect us, in some way, to those holidays; but that's just the passive part of "being Jewish."

Yet to make "being Jewish" active doesn't require much. You need to be willing to remember, to stir up the soup and let your recollections bubble to the top of your awareness so you can skim them off like *shmaltz* (rendered chicken fat) to spread on a slice of bread. You need to be willing to let your mind hopscotch around, and to let a thought lead you somewhere you can't see coming. You need to be willing to ask the questions that have always seemed not to have answers, and to challenge the answers that have always been unsatisfying. You need to be willing to open up, jump in and get messy, to engage with the particulars of Judaism and its holidays.

Although Jewish holidays are exceedingly rich in symbol and sign, and in meaning and message, these lie dormant, if not totally hidden, for many people. But you can take action to have a more vigorous experience; you can, in fact, become the kiss of the handsome prince that awakens the Snow White of your Jewishness. As you think about a holiday, or a particular practice associated with it, grab any little burst of energy or awareness that catches your attention and hang onto it, think on it, follow it where it leads, and try to make it yours. That, in overview, is what this book is about: showing you how engaging with the particulars of the Jewish holidays can lead to new and lively connections, as it did for me — and, perhaps, encouraging you to do it, too.

I hope that you will feel sufficiently inspired and empowered to let yourself have your own encounter with the holidays and their components. Whether those encounters produce writing — or ideas for a painting, or a song, or "just" a new appreciation or understanding of the holiday — is unimportant. What is important is engaging with material, even if it's familiar to you, in a vital, conscious way. There's a long-standing tradition in Judaism of exploring aspects of texts in search of meaning and an explanation of something that's not usually understood: It's called *midrash*. This work has felt midrashic to me, and I encourage you to find your own way to try it.

There are several other ways in which I've imagined you might use this book. You might use it to incorporate some of these readings into the fabric of a holiday service; many congregations use what are commonly called "additional" or "supplementary" readings. You might refer to a particular holiday's readings before going to services, to prepare yourself for the service, or read them after you return home, as a way to continue and lengthen the spirit of that holiday. If you don't go to services but want to recognize and somehow mark a holiday, maybe these readings will speak to you. Or you might bring this book to synagogue with you and leaf through it at times in the service that call for individual meditation.

Although I've tried to use correct facts, in no way do I think my interpretations and reactions to each holiday are "right." And you might not like, understand, or approve of some of my poems to or about God (in which case I am sorry, but that's what I was thinking or feeling at a particular time in my life.) What follows are my own particular perspectives on these holidays, some of which might sound familiar or true to you. My hope, as you go through the book, is that you'll think, "Oh, I've always wondered about that," or "That's always bothered me, too," or "That's an interesting way to deal with that ritual or that reading."

I've divided this book by the different Jewish holidays (and I did not write about every holiday.) The section for each holiday has within it three types of poems, although not in any particular order: Poems that deal with the holiday's religious rituals, prayers, scripture, and midrash; poems about the customs, foods, practices, and overall spirit of the holiday; and *my own* personal associations, experiences, and ruminations on that holiday. In addition, each holiday's set of poems is preceded by a list of words and phrases integral to that holiday; and there are some poems that require their own particular explanation.

The title of this book, "In the Spirit of the Holidays," refers to the spiritual nature that underlies all the Jewish holidays — but I chose it, too, to demonstrate that actively engaging with the holidays can also be spirited: vital, intentional, and dynamic. The word "spirit" comes from the Latin word for breath; in Hebrew, *neshamah* — soul — comes from *nasham*, to "breathe." You can think of "spirit" as a life-giving force that endows a body with energy and power. So take a deep breath and come along to tangle with the holidays.

ACKNOWLEDGMENTS

Acknowledgments

I started writing these poems in the late 1980s, so this collection has been in the works for many years.

I am grateful to Rabbi Vivian Schirn, the founding rabbi of Or Hadash: A Reconstructionist Congregation, of Fort Washington, Pa., and Rabbi Elliot Holin, the founding rabbi of Congregation Kol Ami of Elkins Park, Pa., for encouraging and enthusing about my writing and asking me to read my poems at various synagogue services.

Thanks to Annette Murray, a supportive and knowledgeable book "midwife," who guided me through the process of getting this book ready for publication.

I'd like to thank these friends and relatives who read some of the poems and gave me their feedback: Phyllis Actman, Jonathan Atkins, Dana Axelrod, Sharon Barr, Denise Baum, Riva Blumenfeld, Donna Brian, Barry Brian, Julie Cohen, Natalie Dyen, Joyce Eisenberg, Reena Sigman Friedman, Linda Hansell, Carol Hupping, Betti Kahn, Miriam Kahn, David Monblatt, Lynn Rosen, Shelley Rosenberg, Karyn Scher, Rebecca Schwartz, Bob Seltzer, Betty Shapiro, Bill Shapiro, Phil Straus, and Mark Swartz.

Thanks, also, to Miriam Kahn, Martha Mott-Gale, and Sharon Barr, for proofreading the last pre-published version of this book.

Cheryl Magen, who coached me for my bat mitzvah in 1984 and is one of my dearest friends, not only read and commented on some poems but was a reliable and generous source of information.

Special thanks to Ellen Cassedy, Roz Holtzman, and Michael Krass for reading and providing incisive, well-informed, and challenging input about a greater share of the poems.

ACKNOWLEDGMENTS

My friend, Jonathan Harmon, was an amazing help, reading all the poems of several holidays, then sitting with me in my office as we worked through any changes; he is both sensitive to the meaning and sounds of words, and knowledgeable about a wide range of Jewish topics. And we had a great time working together.

My husband, Cary Mazer, was both the first — and last — person to read most of these poems. He has enthusiastically supported this project from the get-go (even when I was writing about things in our life that were personal and sometimes painful.) Cary has also been my soulmate through the twists and turns of our spiritual wanderings.

Also, thanks to my daughter, Hope Falon-Mazer, a terrific young woman who seems to understand that sometime I have to hide out in my office rather than cheering her on at soccer games.

Special Acknowledgment

I'm grateful to my friend Joyce Eisenberg, and to Ellen Scolnic, for their book, *JPS Dictionary of Jewish Words*, which was an important source as I put together this book. Any time you see a *** notation, it means I've borrowed information, sometimes verbatim, from their book.

In the great majority of cases, I also used the *JPS Dictionary of Jewish Words* as my source for the correct spelling of many Jewish words (although valid variations exist.)

ROSH HASHANAH

Explanation of words, phrases, and concepts appearing in the Rosh Hashanah poems

ROSH HASHANAH is the Jewish New Year, which usually falls sometime in September. It begins the ten-day period of self-reflection and repentance that ends at the last moments of **Yom Kippur**.

Adonai is the most commonly used name for God in prayers.

***Akedah** is the incident in Genesis when God tells Abraham to bind his son Isaac and prepare to sacrifice the boy. At the last moment, God stops Abraham from going through with the deed. Explanations of the **Akedah** include that God was testing Abraham's obedience; that it shows God never would allow human sacrifice; and that God is benevolent, understanding, and respectful of a parent's love for his or her child.

The evocative melody, **Avinu Malkeinu** — traditionally translated as "Our Father, Our King" — is a prayer of supplication: "Our Father, Our King, hear our voice . . . Our Father, Our King, have compassion upon us . . ." It is about our relationship to God, a plea for help and improvement. It can, however, be read in many ways.

For **Azazel**, see **Yom Kippur** explanations.

The **Book of Life** is a "book" in which God writes the names of righteous people. On **Rosh Hashanah**, the book is opened and you have ten days, until the last moment of **Yom Kippur**, when the book is shut, to atone and make things right in your life.

Challah is an egg bread, usually braided and eaten on ceremonial occasions such as **Shabbat** and major Jewish Holidays. On **Rosh Hashanah**, the **challah** may be rolled into a circular shape symbolizing the cycle of the year. (By the way, "*challah* bread" is redundant; *challah* is a bread.)

***Elul** is the last month in the Jewish calendar, falling in August or September, right before the High Holy Days.

For **the four sons,** see Passover explanations.

***Fressing** means eating or snacking, often in large quantities.

On the first day of **Rosh Hashanah**, the traditional Jewish **Torah** reading is Genesis 21. In it, according to Rabbi Arthur Waskow, "Abraham's second wife **Hagar** and his first son Ishmael are sent forth from Abraham's family, with a leather-skin of water that is not enough to meet their needs in the dry wilderness. Hagar gently lays Ishmael beneath a tree and begins to weep as she fears his death. Then, says the **Torah**, Hagar's eyes are opened, and she saw the wellspring that she names 'Be'er Lachai Roi, The Wellspring of the Living ONE who sees me.' It saves their lives."

Elkanah had two wives: **Hannah**, the favorite, who was childless, and Peninnah, who had given birth. Peninnah mocked Hannah because of her infertility, and would take pains to remind her of this difference between them. Hannah prayed to God — the movement of her silent lips misinterpreted as drunkenness — and did eventually give birth to Samuel.

When reciting the words **Kadosh, Kadosh, Kadosh** (holy, holy, holy) in the holiness prayer, we stand with our feet together and rise up on our toes for each repetition, as if to get closer to God.

A **Kohen** is a Jew who can trace his (or her) ancestry to the ancient priestly tribe descended from Aaron.

Left-handedness used to be thought of as a weakness, even a malady.

For *minyan*, see **Purim** explanations.

Moriah is the name given to a mountainous region by the Book of Genesis, in which context it is the location of the sacrifice of Isaac.

Punim is a face.

In Hebrew, **Sarah** means princess. **Isaac** means laughter.

Shabbos is the Yiddish pronunciation of **Shabbat**, or Sabbath.

Shanah tovah means happy new year.

***A **shofar** is a hollowed-out ram's horn that is blown like a trumpet. It is blown on **Rosh Hashanah** and at the end of **Yom Kippur** as part of the prayer services.

For **shul,** see **Purim** explanations.

Sukkot is a holiday. See **Sukkot** poems.

*****Tashlikh** is a ceremony performed on the afternoon of the first day of **Rosh Hashanah.** Jews gather at some flowing source of water and empty their pockets of crumbs (or bring bread crumbs) into the water, casting away sins and transgressions from the past year so to start the new year with a clean slate.

There are **ten days** between **Rosh Hashanah** and **Yom Kippur,** during which time you're supposed to ask for forgiveness and make amends before the Book of Life for the upcoming year is sealed. This can be achieved through repentance, prayers, and charity. The Hebrew word for the concept of repentance is **teshuvah,** which is literally translated as "returning" — the need to see and acknowledge everything of the past year as you move forward into the new year.

Unetaneh Tokef is a dark liturgical poem describing a day of judgment which, for Jews, occurs each year. It includes these lines:

"On *Rosh Hashana*h it is inscribed,
And on *Yom Kippur*, it is sealed.
How many shall pass away and how many shall be born,
Who shall live and who shall die,
Who shall reach the end of his days and who shall not,
Who shall perish by water and who by fire,
Who by sword and who by wild beast,
Who by famine and who by thirst,
Who by earthquake and who by plague . . ."

Wooly Willy is a toy, introduced in 1955, in which metal filings are moved around with a magnetic wand to add features to a cartoon face.

***Definition from the *Dictionary of Jewish Words.*
See **page xxv** for more information.

My New Year

January first doesn't feel like my new year
even though it's time for fresh calendars,
and melancholy after-Christmas sales,
and bracing for icy winter, and wishing for spring,
and starting from zero in Blue Cross deductibles,
and whittling-down diets after holiday *fressing*.

Rosh Hashanah feels like my new year
when even in the fickle weather of late summer
we start to anticipate leaves wearing party dresses,
and kids, bored with freedom, going back to school,
and tans fading
and we all shift inward,
towards the refuge of home,
towards the comfort of heart,
towards the warmth of forgiving each other.

"Your love never fails.
You have always been our hope."

Turn this around.
Turn it inside out.

Talk to yourself:
Say, My own love is a river that never runs dry,
a spelunking flashlight that never dims,
the sun, which shines even when we can't see it.
I am, always.

Say, My own love never fails.
I will not give up on myself.

Repeat as many times as you need
when you think, "not me,
I'm not enough,
I don't have enough."
Remind yourself of giving when you knew nothing
    was left,
of squeezing drops from a dry sponge
of growing sweet tomatoes in the sand.
Remind yourself, yes.

As you start this period of reflection
stand naked before the mirror
and see the eyes-to-your-soul
as well as your neck, the connection between head
    and body,
and the shoulders that have carried
and the back that has borne weight
and the knees that have bent
and the feet planted solid.

See yourself and see good.
See the opportunity for good.
See dedication to better.

Say, My own love never fails.
I will not give up on myself.

"Your love never fails. You have always been our hope." are
lines from the Rosh Hashanah evening service in *The New
Union Prayer Book for the Days of Awe*. They remind me of the
church where my parents' synagogue met, where these words
are written above the cross: Love Never Faileth.

Here I am Again

Here I am again.
This congregation.
This same room. These same prayers.
The same hopes and intentions, mostly, that I bring
  every year.

And yet I keep coming back
for another chance, another opportunity,
another beginning, that maybe this year
will be the one that makes the difference,
that this will be the year when I'm finally able
to cross off the big things from my list,
that I'll do the to-do's
and stop the to-don'ts.

Some years it feels like nothing much is different,
that I'm still stuck on the same old stuff
so the year that's ending must not have mattered.
But it did; if I'm honest with myself
and consider all I've done,
I have moved on, if only a bit.
The year mattered.

After all the High Holy Days I've been through,
I now know that change isn't always big.
For most of us, change doesn't come in neon colors,
  accompanied by an oompah band.
Mostly,
the changes I make are small enough to fit in
  my pocket.
But they're mine,

and along with a candy wrapper and a quarter for
  the meter,
my pocket
this year
is full to overflowing.

Why the
Rosh Hashanah Challah
Is Round

A triangle wouldn't work
or a rectangle, or square.
They're too full of angles
and corners to get stuck in.
They're too eager to settle down
and stay put, unable to move on their own.
They're too solid, and pointed,
with edges that poke and remind.

But the circle works;
so much of life is round:
Wheels, for moving forward,
empty spools, the residue of mending,
a dining room table without a head,
the rings around the glow of Saturn,
pancakes, baby cheeks, jars of jelly,
the hollow of a paper-towel roll,
balls, for batting out of the park,
pies, and buttons that hold things together, and
the smiley "happy face" on a car's rear windshield,
hula hoops, doorknobs, and domes,
the truth of what-goes-around-comes, too,
wedding bands, kaleidoscopes
coins and tick-tocking clocks,
theater in the Shakespeare-type,
fiery hoops for jumping through,
balloons, tires,
and the hole of an O.

A calendar is round, too,
and keeps coming back on itself.
So you can hop on, anywhere,
and go for the ride around time,
another time.

Going Through the Motions

When you stand, I stand.
When you sit, I sit.
When you bow, I bend a tiny little bit.
When you lift yourselves up to *kadosh, kadosh, kadosh*
I watch
and when you stretch out your arm
into the aisle
to touch the Torah
and kiss the book in between
I go through the motions.
And today
the motion that matters most to me
is staying
still,
not following my self out the door
because nothing is meaning much,
and my faith, today,
is only hope
that one moment will matter,
that I'll connect, once,
to why I'm here
like chaotic shards of metal waiting to be magnetized
and formed into shape, like Wooly Willie's beard.
I'm dying to connect, once.
So I wait
for I'm not sure what,
going through the motions
and staying, still
as you stand
and sit
and rock
and bow down low

I wait, still,
going through the motions
even though, in truth,
I'm gone.

The Minute the Melody Starts

Avinu Malkeinu is the prayer
that made my mother cry
because it reminded her of asking for impossible
   things
from her father
knowing he couldn't
or wouldn't.

Avinu Malkeinu is the prayer
that makes many people cry
because it makes them feel helpless
and reminds them of asking for impossible things
from their parents
knowing they couldn't
or wouldn't.

No matter how we change the words
from "our father, our king"
to "our guardian, our ruler,"
Avinu Malkeinu is still the prayer
that reminds me it's not any parent
who has to improve the world
and create a good year —
It's me
even if I can't
or won't

and maybe it's because of this,
because I can flip it
from passivity into possibility,
that *Avinu Malkeinu* is a prayer
of power, and no,
I don't cry.

Fall

Fall
is when my octogenarian friend Fred comes back to
    the gym after swimming at his condominium pool
    club all summer
and we kiss good-to-see-you, how-are-you
and I lie, and tell him I'm okay,
and I wonder, aloud, if he's lost weight, or gotten a
    haircut, or something.
"I'm a pig," he says. "I have to lose five pounds."
Dear Fred — who swims with his glasses on, his head
    always above water —
who I sometimes want to ask to stand in for my
    father,
now that he's gone.
Fred asks me, again, if I'm Jewish,
— "come on, look at this *punim*," I respond —
and he nods
and we wish each other a *shanah tovah*
and a healthy one
and a sweet one.

I love the old people who swim at my pool;
they don't know how much they hold me up.
I go back to my laps
back and forth,
I'm counting,
and I'm thinking, maybe I should go over to lane five
and say, Fred, I lied to you,
I'm suffering,
I'm in a lot of pain,
and I'm not having a happy new year.
Will you hug me, please?

and he would,
like Dolly, who also uses the pool for praying,
and Bea, who embroidered pillowcases for us after
 we'd lost the baby,
and Lee, who gets lonely for far-away family on the
 holidays, too,

and this all makes me feel
that I *do* belong somewhere
and that in the pool
the hand I'm dying to hold
is under me, supporting me aloft,
letting me collapse into afloat.

Services

Sometimes I wonder why am I here
with you, what I'm hoping will happen
if I'm in this room with you, what I imagine
could happen in this room with you.
My friend, I come here from longing to be
with you, even though I've never shaken your hand,
that being in this room with someone like you
— someone I don't know but others I know do —
will somehow lift me from my day and make
   me lighter
and I'll fly like a Chagall lover through wisps of clouds
over my life, over all I've ever done, and when I do
I'll see that it all adds up to something,
that somewhere you might have played a part
even if we hadn't been introduced,
even if I hadn't yet learned your name.

God Writes in the Book of Life

He holds his pen funny,
uses a Mont Blanc knock-off that he bought
from a street hawker off Times Square,
with a lifetime supply of black ink
and an eraser he never uses.

He writes in a marble composition book
instead of on the wall, like he used to.
His cursive is illegible
so he prints like a second-grader
and his shorthand is even worse.

He uses his left hand
in spite of being hit with a ruler by the teacher,
and the graphologists say
he's someone who craves control, attention,
and is quick to judge.

Where We End Up: Unetaneh Tokef

There's a lot of space
between who shall live
and who shall die;
a lot of air
separating tranquil and troubled,
and distance from rich to poor.

Just as there are ten days
dividing written from sealed,
so do we need to recognize the space
between sinner and saint,
bad and good,
loser and winner.
It's unlikely we'll find ourselves
in the whorls, and the mucky-black hole
or, at the other extreme,
at the golden-glass distance beyond the horizon.

Most of us will end up in the middle,
pedaling a unicycle
with one arm reaching forward,
the other, back,
balancing, mostly, nicely,
on our way to as far as we can see.

God Bless My Cats

I am grateful to Yankel, my marmalade cat,
a 25-pounder who loved only me,
the first cat I ever cared for on my own,
for teaching me that grief
— jagged, unpredictable, interminable grief,
thief of sleep and appetite —
does, in fact, end.

Even though I was 42, I didn't know about grief when
    he died;
Yankel was the first being I ever lost who mattered.
I'm self-conscious to admit that, because my four
    grandparents had died by then, when I was young.
But they were unhappy, sour people,
immigrants with their own thick language
which no one thought to translate for me.
They barely escaped the Old Country with their lives,
let alone any dreams
or ancestral *Shabbos* candlesticks.
I never felt much with or for them.
President Kennedy died when I was a child, around
    the same time.
But that was different, a bigger loss, the loss of safety
    and trust,
And Kennedy was a head loss for me, not a heart loss.

Loss is worst when it's someone you live with:
It's the death of daily rituals, sharing food or the
    bathroom sink, feeling the other's breath nearby
    at night.

It's the loss of moments of sweet talk, connections
  of touch,
and the disappearance of a presence, a heartbeat —
  even silent — in the next room.

It was late summer when Yankel died,
early in the month of *Elul*,
when summer and fall play tag, take turns
and I know that certain plants in my backyard won't
  survive until *Sukkot*.
When he died, I thought I would, too.
Trite, but in the middle of nightsleep
I felt I would drown in raging waves of grief,
that I would be sucked under, again and again,
thrashed about in the dark, the unknown deep.
Even my husband, a lifeguard when young, couldn't
  save me,
and I went under until sunrise,
emerging spent, thirsty, and gritty with sand.

I can't recall how long it took until I could float again,
until I didn't worry about being swallowed by
  the waves,
but one day I realized I was just sad,
no longer held under by rusting fetters of grief,
and I didn't have to fear feeling.

Each loss is different,
but when my father died, five years later,
I didn't dread the undertow.
I trusted the grief would subside.
I knew I would survive.

Before I lived with cats, a wise woman taught me,
    "The only way out is through."
Yes.
Enduring my cat's death showed me that if I fell,
    sooner or later I would,
cat-like,
land on my feet.

Yankel, and now two others, are buried in our
    backyard.
I greet them when I go out there, pulling weeds that
    spread like ferny fingers over their stones.
I'm grateful for what they taught me
even as they're a few feet down, their stones warming,
    cat-like, in the sun.

What God Is

I realized what God is
the other morning
when my cat jumped up on the sink
to drink from the faucet
after he'd been listless
and unresponsive for days
and I thought he might be dying.

So I turned on the water
and he drank big gulps
and I thanked God.
And when my husband yelled up from the kitchen
    that the Friskies were gone
I thanked God, again.
And it came to me
in one big gulp,
that sometimes,
God is when things go my way.

Grammar

"To be" is passive:
I am. You are.
He is. She is.
We are. They are.
(And "you are," once again, in the plural.)

"To be" sits there
like a couch potato guzzling beer.
It waits for someone else to do something,
to take a stand,
then heavily hoists itself up from the couch
and takes a clumsy step.
Then, if it's not too sloshed, "to be" will respond
and move where you want it to go.

But sometimes "to be" is too dull,
too listless, too lazy,
to do much of anything.

"To be" needs "to do."
"To be" free, for example, requires acts of freedom:
Sitting down, solid and square, in the prohibited part
   of the bus,
standing on a picket line demonstrating against
   injustice,
striding with a crowd protesting yet another bad war.

"To be" anything, anyone
— a good Jew,
a creative, patient parent,
a friend for the long run,
(even a writer who wants to move you) —

"to be" needs to be preceded by action,
always
in all ways.

To become what you want "to be,"
the first step is "to do."

"Blessed is the Eternal our God, who has made me *to be* free"
is from *The New Union Prayer Book for the Days of Awe*.

Which Is Why She Is Blowing Shofar With Sid

He's about to retire.
She's not the retiring type,
which is why
    unlike his profession
    she doesn't believe
    in holding on to the past,
which is why
she is learning
to blow air
through a ram's horn
(even though, as a vegetarian, she doesn't
  quite approve.)

He holds it loosely from the side of his mouth,
a Chicago gangster cigar.
She holds it fervently, straight out, and down,
a reflective tenor sax,
which is why
    unlike his plans
    she isn't traveling
    anywhere,
which is why
she is learning
to gather people
with an animal's wordless cry
(even though, as a writer, she doesn't quite trust
  the wordlessness.)

He has already made his sounds,
had his turn,
landing on target each time.

She, for the first time, will take aim
and make sound,
her turn at last
which is why

> She is blowing *shofar* with Sid
> and taking turns,
> not concerned with erasing his mouth from the
> ram's horn,

but learning
how to place her mouth
and breathe her life through the tunnel
and create a powerful sound
(even though, as a woman, she wishes it didn't quite
    matter so much)
which is
why

It's only been in the past few decades that women were
permitted — let alone encouraged — to blow *shofar*. My friend,
the late Sid Altman, a psychiatrist who was about to retire, gave
me my first lesson.

Hagar's Eyes Were Opened

and she looked around the desert
and saw what had been there, always:
A well filled with lifesource,
the answer, for now, for her thirst,
so she drank,
and her son drank,
and everything was a-okay.

I was going to pray for the ability to discern
the hidden well in my own desert ramblings
which would have been nice —
but I don't trust, right now,
that you're there to pull aside the curtain
so I'll be able to see.

So here's what I'm going to give myself,
what I'm not waiting to get from you:
The power to open my own eyes
and the strength to dig my own well.

Leave It to a Woman

It was Hannah, the graceful one,
who first used words to talk upward
instead of writing with the blood of speechless
    beasts.

It was Eli, the *Kohen* steeped in wine,
who thought she was drunk
instead of being overcome with her need to speak up.

It was *Adonai,* the embodiment of ears,
who first listened to the movement of her lips
instead of hearing just the animals' cry.

A traditional Bible reading for Rosh Hashanah is the story of
Hannah, who prays to God for a child and is rewarded with the
birth of Samuel. This is an example of using words, rather than
animal sacrifice, to reach God.

Tashlikh: And You Shall Cast All Your Sins Into the Depths of the Sea

Hansel and Gretel left behind breadcrumbs,
hoping to find their way home
and out of the forest.
We, too, with intentions,
discard pieces of stale bread — old Wonder, maybe —
but we hope we won't go down those same
    paths again:
       This hunk for selfishness.
       Another for intolerance.
       One more for dishonesty.
We watch them float down free-flowing water,
away and under, under and away.
Breaking bread and tossing it
feeds the autumn-grown ducks
and so reminds us of the act of relinquishing,
of giving up and making space,
of letting go what's fueled us in the past
      and hoping it will be transformed into someone
      else's food.

Barren

Look it up in your Roget's:
Ineffectual.
Bare.
Unimaginative.
Dull.
And especially, under Unproductive:
Fruitless
and Unfruitful.
Infecund.
Sterile and Impotent
  (which make you feel more like a man)
Childless.
Without issue.

Banish the word
to wander the wilderness of Beersheba
or *Azazel*
with Hagar or the goat,
Strike it out,
slash it away,
render it invisible —
just like the status of barren women.

If

If instead of sending away Hagar
and her son to the wildness of Beersheba,
with woolly bushes and bread and a skin of water,
Sarah, the Princess, could have asked for her advice:
How to bathe Isaac, the Laughing One,
what to do when he cries with closed-tight fists,
when to call someone about his colic.
Hagar could have passed down Ishmael's
    outgrown clothes,
shared secrets for bringing on sleep,
offered a poultice for sore nipples, another for
    tender gums.

If instead of lauding her fecundity over Hannah, the
    Graceful One,
who, in desperation, promised her first-born son
    to God,
Peninah, the Pearl, would have listened, and quietly
    held her hand,
spoken words of patience and sympathy from the
    Circle of Women,
and reminded Hannah she could adopt
(and by the way, the baby didn't have to be a boy.)

If instead of comparing the number of infant
    silhouettes on a charm bracelet
or complaining, but not really, about all the work of
    child-raising
and competing in Womanhood based on issues of
    the womb,

they felt for each other
and mothered each other
and played each other's daughter.

Note: I wrote this when I was feeling betrayed, angry, grief-stricken, and disillusioned, thus my strong language.

Why I'm Not Doing Tashlikh This Year

I'm angry with you, God.
You tricked me into thinking life is fair
and that if I did good things,
God things,
I'd get what I deserved,
what I'd hoped for
(which wasn't so extraordinary,
just basic things like everyone else.)

But you tricked me, God,
dangling what I wanted in front of me, then snatching
   it away when I thought it was mine.
And now you expect me to take the crumbs from my
   pocket and toss them,
my misdeeds and regrets,
into flowing waters? I won't.
I don't have anything to give.
Loss after loss has diminished me
and I'm tired and small;
I need to hang on to what little I have.
Of course I've made mistakes,
but it's your turn, God, this year,
to atone
and admit
and commit to making better.
You owe me, God, big time.

Yes, I'm furious.
Today, rather than going to *shul*,
I should have gone swimming,

where I usually can feel your big daddy hand
holding me up when I give in,
and give up the fight,
flat on my back,
and trust you won't let me down, or drown.

But I didn't, God. Silly me.
I thought I'd visit you and try again.
(I hope you know that the fact I was there
means I haven't given up, not totally,
not yet.)

So here's what I want, today;
I want this instead of *tashlikh*:
I want you to make it rain.
I want you to take the waters that you've sucked up
   during this long, scorched, yellow summer
and pour them down on me.
I'm parched, God. I could be dying.
I want you to rain down the waters that might have
   been the stream I'd *tashlikh* into,
and make it flow,
abundant and life-bearing.
I want you to write little fortune-cookie messages
— apologizing to me,
forecasting only good things —
and have them wash up on the shore
where I can collect them and paste them
into my journal.

On this day when other people are discarding pieces
  of themselves
I want the holes in me filled.

Sarah, Barren, Bears Fruit

She is no longer a young woman.
Blood still flows, but less red, less rich,
and finally, she understands
and starts laughing.

As she opens her mouth
a branch issues forth
as if from her belly,
covered with little crackly leaves and
    blood-red apples,
firm, and imperfectly round and shiny
as if polished by hand.

She laughs, delighted, and looks down
and sees her legs become a pear-tree trunk
planted firmly,
and when she wiggles her roots with joy
more than a minyan of fruit fall
unbruised, perfectly ripe.

She laughs, amazed,
and when she lifts her arms
they become branches of an orange tree,
laden, heavy, ready to be plucked.
And from the tips of her fingers spring clusters
    of grapes
more purple than red, with seeds.

She laughs, loving this change of life,
and from her belly button creep tomato vines
with oval plums
the perfect red

while her nipples burst
bearing clementines
that she will gift to every child she knows.

She laughs,
at last,
and her fruit shakes like a windstorm.
When pieces fall
she is replenished,
and when she squats with her weight
she bears honeydew,
sweet,
ripe,
fleshy,
perfect.

Questions for the Akedah (Binding)

Pardon me for questioning, but
where the hell was Sarah?
Why didn't Abraham tell her his plans?
For that matter, why didn't God?

I have an answer, that maybe I wouldn't have had
     before having a child:
Because they knew her mother's-love would have
     made her
kidnap their son and lock him up somewhere,
somewhere safe, some womb, to which she had the
     only key.
She would have sharpened her fingers to talons
and fought,
a raptor ripping off her husband's flesh
to keep him from taking their son
to that place, *Moriah*,
that place that Abraham names, "The Lord Sees."

If that's seeing, I'd just as soon be blind.

And why didn't Isaac fight back,
kicking, scratching, biting Abraham,
screaming for his life?
Did he plead, wail, or howl like a dark forest night,
or was he silent, or drugged,
or like one of Passover's Four Sons,
was he "slow-witted"?

I want to know:
Did Abraham weep as he tied up his son?
Did he think, "take me instead"?

Did he say that aloud?
Shouldn't he?
If I were Abraham, I would have lived in fear;
even though I'd been promised many descendants,
powerful descendants,
the moon and the stars and a golden path,
what next atrocity would I be forced to perform to
   prove my faith?

Later,
if I were Sarah, I would have left Abraham,
left him for his secrecy,
his passivity, his unwillingness to question.
What kind of man would have brought that blade so
   close?

If I were Isaac, I would find another flock.
I'd cut out my father, never be with him again.

And if I were God, I would have wondered
— as I recalled the glint of sun on silver —
I would have wondered, what have I done?

Confusion

One year,
when summer stretched beyond its boundaries
and I was nine, my next-door friend and I
   got confused.
On *Rosh Hashanah* we sat solemn, dark, and stiff,
and on *Yom Kippur*, we played, loud, sweaty, and hard.

No one noticed.

No neighbors tattled to our parents, and neither of us
   was punished.
We weren't struck down, either, as we feared.
But when I realized our mistake, and felt ashamed,
I knew I'd learned an important lesson:
The only one keeping score is me.

The Bridge Between Rosh Hashanah and Yom Kippur

It's a long bridge, and high,
steep, and it sways with the wind.
Its pilings lie deep in the water,
dug into the foundation of earth.

It takes ten days to cross by foot
— you've got to push harder if you're burdened
   with baggage —
and you have to walk it yourself.
No one can carry you.

People have been known to jump off
with the effort of crossing
and the pull of gravity.
They always survive,
and hopefully, try again
the following year.

Each person decides
how many times to pay the toll
and to whom
along the way.
You pay with words:
"I forgive you."
"Please forgive me."

But what's most amazing
is that you're supposed to keep turning around
as you walk,
turning around
to face all four corners

and everything in between,
turning around
to make sure you've seen every person
and the vista of your past year
so you can pay up and start fresh
on the other side.

Instead of getting dizzy
as you cross
you feel lighter, and cleaner,
more at-one with yourself
and all the other travelers.

When you reach the other side,
and feel the earth, solid beneath your feet,
you'll know
you've arrived —
weary yet grateful,
renewed and ready.

YOM KIPPUR

Explanation of words, phrases, and concepts appearing in the Yom Kippur poems

***YOM KIPPUR, also known as the **Day of Atonement**, is the most solemn day on the Jewish calendar. It is a day to fast and pray in the synagogue, and marks the culmination of the ten-day period of self-examination, repentance, and prayer.

***__Kol Nidre__ is the name of the synagogue service on the night of *Yom Kippur*. It is also an ancient prayer recited in synagogue at that service, sung in a distinctive, haunting melody in keeping with the spirit of the holiday.

In the prayer, one asks to be excused and released from vows made but not kept during the past year and in the new year to come.

Tradition says that *Yom Kippur* is the day on which God will seal the fate of every Jew. Traditionally, the Book of Life is opened for the righteous on *Rosh Hashanah* so that God can inscribe their names. The fate of all other people is on hold until the last moment of *Yom Kippur*, when God closes the Book of Life having determined the quality of their coming year.

The *Torah* reading for *Yom Kippur* explains, in detail, how Aaron is supposed to prepare a sin offering, part of which includes sending a goat — the original scapegoat — into the wilderness, into **Azazel**. But no description of *Azazel* is given.

Bruce Springsteen is — Of COURSE you know who he is!

Daven means to pray.

***__Fapitzed__ means all dolled up; overdressed for the occasion.

Between *Rosh Hashanah* and *Yom Kippur*, you're supposed to ask **forgiveness** of people you may have wronged in the past year, and to forgive people who ask that of you.

The High Holidays — or High Holy Days — refers to *Rosh Hashanah*, *Yom Kippur*, and the days in between.

***Kaparos** is an old-fashioned ritual, performed on *Yom Kippur* eve, when a person would swing a chicken over his or her head three times while praying for his or her sins to be forgiven. It was a way to symbolically transfer those sins and transgression to another object (a "scapegoat" action.) I always wondered what happened to the chicken afterwards; I would have not wanted to eat it. Not surprisingly, I wrote *This is my Substitute, this is my Atonement: Kaparot* when I was a vegetarian.

According to Hasidic practice, however, the rite consists of taking a chicken and gently passing it over the head of each family member three times while reciting the appropriate text. The fowl is then slaughtered in accordance with Kosher procedures and its monetary worth given to the poor, or as is more popular today, the chicken itself is donated to a charitable cause.

One essential *Yom Kippur* prayer incorporates a long, communal confession of a long list of sins, and some people lightly **knock on their chest** — the house of the heart — with each sin. When you admit your wrongdoings as part of a synagogue community, you not only help yourself move beyond your "sins," but doing this along with other people doing the same thing feels very unifying, very democratic.

****Nachas** means fulfillment, proud pleasure, special joy, especially in the accomplishments of one's children or grandchildren.

Rabbi Menachem Mendel Schneerson, leader of the **Lubavitcher Hasidic** movement, was one of the most influential Jewish leaders of the 20th-century.

For **rise up on their tiptoes** during the *Kedushah* prayer, see *Rosh Hashanah* explanations.

Shmeer is something you spread on a bagel, usually cream cheese.

Tallis is the Yiddish pronunciation of the Hebrew word *tallit*, a large rectangular prayer shawl made of wool, cotton, or synthetic fibers. In each of the four corners of the shawl are strings tied in a particular pattern, called *tzitzit*.

The **Tin Man** is the character in *The Wizard of Oz* who wants a heart.

For *Torah,* see *Simchat Torah* explanations.

Yad Vashem is the Holocaust history museum and archives in Israel.

***Yizkor* is a special memorial prayer recited for a deceased member of the immediate family. It is recited in synagogue on *Yom Kippur*, as well as three other holidays. Because of superstition, children with parents who are still living often leave the sanctuary when *Yizkor* prayers are recited, so as not to tempt the evil eye by participating in a memorial service.

***Definition from the *Dictionary of Jewish Words*. See **page xxv** for more information.

My Confession

I used to think
    that when I was beating my chest with my fist
    it was because I'd been bad
    was guilty
    and was trying to create a physical reminder
    of all I'd done wrong.

I used to think
    that when I was beating my chest with my fist
    it was because, like the Tin Man, there was
        nothing inside
    and I needed to hear the emptiness reverberate
    to remind myself of the hollowness of my
        mortal life
    and how I needed to fill the emptiness,
        each year,
    with the viscera of good intentions.

Now I know
    that when I'm beating my chest with my fist
    it is because I'm knocking on the door to
        my heart
    I'm gaining access
    and entrance
    to the pink, warm part of me
    hoping to release the love
    and forgiveness
of my self.

The Responsibility of a Goat

Azazel is midnight
blue, cliffs and rocks,
Columbus edges,
every step unsure.

Azazel is noon
time sun, too yellow to believe,
it dries you, a parchment of lies,
makes corners shrivel and curl.

Azazel is dinner
time for predators, deprived,
pouncing off haunches, claws sharpened on glass,
mouths rounded into screams.

Azazel is morning, wailing,
stubble of tarnished hope,
endless, always,
the undiscovered planet without footsteps.

But why should a goat, however sure-footed,
have to wander?

Today,
instead of the goat,
I go to *Azazel*
myself.

At-one-ment

Every day should be the day of atonement
if you think of today
as the day of at-one-ment.
    At-one-ment means being close to your center
        your core
        your essence
    At-one-ment means knowing what's important
        what's meaningful
        what can be let go of
    At-one-ment means acknowledging your
      unique values
        your links to humanity
        your own roadblocks to overcome
    At-one-ment means identifying your center
      of power
        to change
        to grow
        to evolve
    At-one-ment means reaching towards godliness
        knowing your limitations
        pushing beyond your boundaries
At-one-ment means achieving at-one-ness
  with yourself
every day
starting today
this day
of at-one-ment.

Why I Fast

I fast because I'm supposed to
I fast because I'm afraid not to
I fast because I don't want that to be the reason I don't
   get sealed in The Book
I fast because I don't want that to be the reason The
   Gate closes before I slip in
I fast because God wants me to
I fast in case there is God

I fast because I want to prove to myself that I
   have discipline
I fast because I want to show myself I'm not a slave
   to food
I fast because I want to demonstrate that I have
   mastery over my desires
I fast because I have the ability to concentrate on
   things other than my animal self
I fast to see if I can
I fast because it's no big deal

I fast because food tastes sweeter after
I fast because I eat too much in anticipation of
   this fast
I fast to punish myself because I've sinned
I fast because I want to see if lack of food makes me
   feel spiritual
I fast because it makes me feel clean
I fast because not eating gives me more time to be in
   the spirit of *Yom Kippur*

I fast because I always have
I fast because everyone else does
(and those who don't keep it quiet)
I fast in solidarity with people who've fasted
   throughout history
I fast because the rest of my community is fasting
I fast because I feel virtuous later when I tell people
   I've fasted
I fast because I'd be embarrassed to tell people
   I hadn't

I fast because
I fast.

Why I Don't Fast

How can I focus inward
on my spirit
my heart
my head
if all I hear are the growls of my animal need,
the rumblings of grinding against emptiness
and the wavy churnings of want?

I can force myself to push beyond the voice of my
    physical body
and listen to the airier voice that rises
and merges
and mingles like the everywhere smoke of Memorial
    Day barbecues
but this eats up energy I might otherwise use
more wisely
on other matters that matter more.

And after all,
the belly is the source of breath,
and inspiration,
and power,
all that hibernates under the skin of hunger.

I'd rather pray fortified,
my body satisfied,
planted solidly on the ground like an old apple tree
    so I can leave it behind and soar
    aware that I've already compromised
    and am, therefore, deliciously human.

Floyd, and Faith

We lost a tree in the hurricane last week,
an old dogwood, dying anyway,
and we'd been warned that a big wind might take
   it down.
That happened three days before *Yom Kippur*,
with a cleaving sound
like ripping apart the flesh
of a corrugated cardboard box.
In the tree's trunk
was a lot of emptiness,
its root system long dead and dry,
its passages collapsed.
We'll miss the tree
for the privacy it provided
between our house and our neighbors',
and for the soft, pink flowers that still bloomed
on one side of the tree
like the half of a body unfelled by a stroke.

Who will miss it even more are the birds
who used it for shelter
and as a launch pad down to the bird feeder
and a retreat from fights and squabbles.

But who will miss the tree most
are the squirrels
who fed on the bird feeder's overflow.
Now, without the tree,
and the birds,
and their seeds that fell to the ground,
the squirrels seem distressed
and confused.

They're eating differently to fill their bellies
— sucking out the guts of green tomatoes —
and their voices, these days, sound frantic.
They're searching for what they'd come to expect
and what had been there for them
easily, and lazily, as if they were entitled.

I understand.
I understand what it's like to lose your source
   of succor
and to go through the motions
even though you know, you can feel,
that your mother's milk has all of a sudden
   stopped flowing.
My mother went out in a hurricane, once,
to stake up a tree that stands, still.
I need to go out in the storm next time
to try and make sure nothing gets sucked out of life,
to make sure nothing upsets the balance,
so that everything that needs nourishment
gets some.

Hurricane Floyd was a powerful hurricane that struck the east
coast of the United States on September 7-19, 1999.

The Color of Yom Kippur

The color of *Yom Kippur* is grey:
a blend of good and bad
a balance of striving and acceptance
a mixture of angel and human nature.

None of us is so bad
that we don't deserve to forgive ourselves
and try, again, tomorrow,
and none of us will ever achieve the purity of
    today's intentions.

None of us can ever know in how many ways,
and how many times,
we've hurt the people in our lives,
and none of us will ever know all the things we did or
    said which, however small,
pleased others.

None of us is flawed beyond repair
None of us will ever achieve perfection.

We try
We backslide
We forget
We promise
We get too busy
We make lists
        and resolutions
        and mistakes
We despair
and once in a while, we achieve the spark of matching
    deed with intention.

We are all human
not black
not white
but holy
        wholly
        holey
grey.

Wearing Sneakers and White

I

(These wardrobe guidelines will not go over well
in a place where people get *fapitzed*
in gold and fur and understated neutrals
to show off
and tell
of their five-star children accomplishing
and their grandchildren increasing,
and the *nachas* that comes their way
and catches on,
like lint to a half of Velcro.)

II

The truth is,
you're not supposed to wear leather
so we're all equal:
Not you in your Ballys, and your Christian Laboutins
   with their red soles,
and me in slip-ons from Payless that fall apart
— unglue, really — after four exposures to rain.
Sneakers used to democratize us
until they went upper crust
and leather replaced canvas,
and now Air Jordans are a different genus
let alone species,
from the Keds we wore as kids.

If you can find sneakers
not made from the skin of animals,
they're a wise and fitting choice
for the holy day.

Because sneakers support you
and hold you up
so you can go the distance,
and cushion you from unnecessary pebbles and
    annoyances
that would otherwise keep you from staying on track
and get in your way.

III

The other truth is,
you're supposed to wear white,
like a bride,
on this day when you deny yourself
food, and drink.
But for some people
color is nourishment:
A winter coat in highlighter-pink,
the nailpolish-red overalls,
a sweater, the same purple as ring-box velvet.
Some people feel lost in white, and bland,
and almost transparent, like dried Elmer's glue.
They don't realize there's color in white
if you break it down,
and like a peacock who teases
and never fans out his tail,
the color wheel explosion lies rich and dormant
and ripe, inside the spectrum.
Some people don't see the beauty in white:
fresh unruled paper, the shells of eggs,
daisy petals whether he loves me or not,
cat bellies, and snow before the cars come through.
Wearing white is all colors

and none,
like the all-or-nothing promises
and vows of this holy day,
which makes it the perfect color,
the wise and fitting choice.

Another Word for Forgive is Acquit

Today

As we ponder other people
we're supposed to forgive those
who have wronged us,
and be forgiven by them, right or wrong.
We're supposed to consider ourselves part of a
    flawed community
and reconsider its flaws, and our part.

As we assess ourselves
we're meant to wipe the slate clean
and hope for a slate that will need less cleaning
    next year,
admit responsibility for our actions
        and lack of actions,
and vow to act more responsibly next year.

We should, we're taught,
look inward
and draw upon an unlimited reserve of absolution,
an untapped oil well of dismissal,
a Stone Soup of replenishing pardons,
and act as if we've forgiven
(if not forgotten.)

But let's be human:
It doesn't always work
— no matter what day it is —
with all the shoulds on our head.
If something is so wrong,
so in-your-face evil,
so unjust to an innocent goat,

maybe it shouldn't be forgiven,
no matter what day it is
and all the shoulds on our head.

Sometimes
Yom Kippur falls, unintentional and clumsy,
    on the wrong date
and we can't forgive,
and maybe we never will,
and maybe we shouldn't,
and we have to forgive ourselves for that.

Unfortunately,
if you look it up,
another word for forgive is set free.

Ronald Goldman and Nicole Brown Simpson were murdered on
June 12, 1994. O.J. Simpson was found innocent of the crime.

This is my Substitute,
This is my Atonement: Kaparos

If we think
a chicken is big enough
to embody what about us is bad
then we need a bigger bird
because we haven't accounted
for being brutal to God's creatures.

Telling ourselves
that chickens are stupid
and senseless
doesn't make up for it.

Killing the chicken ritually
quickly and cleanly
doesn't make up for it.

Doing it at dawn
before the late sleepers arise
and see
doesn't make up for it.

Leaving out the liver
and the kidney
and the guts
for the birds
doesn't make up for it.

If we think
God will do better by us
not only in spite of,

but because
we've brutalized a living being

that breathes
and experiences in its own unknown way,
then we're disrespecting
not only the beast
but, by golly,
God.

I wrote this poem when I was a vegetarian.

Deaf

Do you remember when,
as a child,
pondering those big questions,
you shared with a friend:
"Would you rather be blind or deaf?"

If I lost my hearing
one of the sounds I would miss most
would be the music of *Kol Nidre*.
It's not Mozart, which moves me,
or West Side Story, or even the raw, early Beatles,
but there's something about the sounds of that night:
The prayer,
its melody so dark and heavy and steplike,
moving up and down stairs, one at a time,
like a toddler teetering between stand and fall.

I hear all the voices of people who've sung it
throughout my life
— and around my life —
because *Kol Nidre* wraps around you like your
    grandfather's *tallis*
and embraces you in its welcome melancholy,
whispering the same indigo secret in each
    person's ear
that yes, you are here,
you are here.

Kol Nidre When My Daughter Isn't Quite Five

Hope, my daughter, you are my *tallis*,
both you and it in stripes and white,
its strings, your blue-black hair.
Sweaty with a touch of fever,
you wrap yourself around me
as we all chant *Kol Nidre*,
and I feel full
in a way that fasting won't affect.

You are the *Torah* Daddy holds,
surprisingly heavy with years
and filled with wisdom to unfurl.
He holds you while weary of standing
but feels strong and constant
in a way that fasting won't affect.

Nothing can change this:
We are satisfied.

On the Night I Stomped Out of Kol Nidre Services

I am at-one-ment
even though I severed myself from the crowd.
They were calm, like floating fish,
sitting back, responding in italics, on cue,
being done for, like the services I had known
and had buried, rotten, forgotten.

I am at-one-ment
even though I hacked myself off from the service,
which was monotone beige,
and flat as death's heartbeat
in an emergency room, like the praying I had known
and had turned off, unwound, shut down.

But I am at-one-ment
    even if I'm alone
with the rings of a tree, the veins of a rock,
and my words, the lump clay for my grappling.

My First Yizkor

It's anticipation
    the same as before I went to *Yad Vashem*
    or Auschwitz
    or even the Holocaust Museum in D.C.
that my emotions will overwhelm me
and I won't be able to "take" it,
although what I really mean by that, I don't know
    That I'll "break down" crying and won't be able
    to stop?
    That I'll drop dead on the spot from the
    intensity?
    That I'll somehow feel so much that I'll burst like
    an overblown balloon, pieces of me scattered
    like an airplane crash over a Pennsylvania field?

It's interesting:
It's only loss
    Jewish loss
that matters, it seems,
that pushes me to the edge of shattering.

Yet at the same time, I'm curious:
It's a rite of passage about something dark,
something I didn't have to deal with when I was
  younger,
    like mammography,
    or mapping out an escape route from my three-
    story home.

        What goes on in there?
        Does everyone weep?
        What words will we say?

Will someone put an arm around me if I
shudder with waves of grief?

This year, it's my time,
my first time, for my father.
So I stuff a tissue up my sleeve,
like my mother does,
and enter to join the others.

Hungry Heart

(With thanks to Bruce Springsteen)

I don't fast well.
Around early afternoon, my stomach gets hot
    and growly.
My head gets woozy, my breath gets wonky, and the
    rest of me feels weak.
I have a hard time thinking about much else other
    than when I'll eat that bagel and *shmeer*, and some
    too-salty fish.

So this year,
instead of focusing on the emptiness of my stomach,
I'm trying to think about the fullness of my heart;
how I can tap into it — like spigoting a sugar maple
    in March —
more quickly, more completely, and with less
    provocation.

At this point in my life, I don't need *Yom Kippur* to tell
    me, in its grandfather-gruff voice, to shape up.
I know that already. I know that every day, maybe
    some days way too much.
But what's the use of acknowledging my
    shortcomings
        and how I've shortchanged people who love or
        need me,
        and been short-sighted in my responses to
        life's complexities
and vowing to improve
if I haven't reminded myself that I have a full heart,
that I can give away while still keeping enough,

that what I give away regenerates like a human liver,
and I rarely reach empty anymore.

Bruce Springsteen,
(who I imagine has been infrequently quoted on
   Yom Kippur)
wrote, "Everybody has a hungry heart."
My heart — thank you, Whoever-You-Are-God,
and thank you, my beloveds — is no longer hungry.
If I listen closely,
its beats — *lub-dub, lub-dub, lub-dub* —
are louder and more reliable
than the temporary rumbles and grumbles of
   my belly.

It's easier to give when you have enough.
But if you try,
you can still drive an extra mile on empty.

Guilty

I remember
when I was young,
being indignant
about including myself with the sinners
who were beating their chests
and confessing to things I didn't understand then,
        like xenophobia and promiscuity.
I'd been a good kid, I thought,
and if I wasn't, my parents would have punished me.

I remember
later,
being relieved
to include myself with the sinners
who were admitting to much
and confessing to things I now knew
        like jealousy and pride.

Now,
I join friends and strangers
and I'm proud to be part of a people
who admit their communal shortcomings
and, once a year, vow to try again, and to do better.

I've stepped into the circle of responsibility
        and if I hadn't,
        that would have been my sin.

Praying in the We

I choose
to join you
to become a we
— like a wedding vow —
a community
of fallible men, women, children,
and innocent babies
who take responsibility for ourselves
who take responsibility for each other
who have, unwittingly,
been for each other:
silent bystander
enabler
unknowing recipient
illicit lover
instigator
grudge-keeper
condoner
judge
promise-breaker
gossip-leaker.
Without knowing,
we have been these things for each other
even if we don't know each other's names.

Yet we are also each other's forgiveness-giver.
So I will try to forgive you
and ask you, the other part of we,
to try and forgive me.

Inner Forgiveness
(Written in my early 20s)

I forgive my parents for not being perfect and all-
    knowing, as I'd believed as a child,
and I forgive my immigrant grandparents for not
    trying to connect to me.

I forgive friends once close with me, who evolved in
    different directions,
and I forgive the special people who told me they'd
    love me forever, then moved on to loving others.

I forgive teachers who told me I didn't have certain
    abilities, whom I believed,
and I forgive the people who helped shape the inner
    boundaries that have kept me back, that I've had to
    work so hard to break beyond.

I forgive business acquaintances who had their
    own agendas and acted differently than I'd have
    preferred,
and I forgive service people who disappointed me and
    not done the job as I'd expected.

I forgive the people who kept me waiting,
    who were lax in giving me what they owed me,
    who were rude and ill-mannered.

I forgive people for their troubled pasts, and I allow
    them to move on and grow.
I forgive the people in my life who act differently than
    I because of their own values.
I forgive people for not being more like me.

I forgive the God-Power for not being able to make
   everything better.

And the most difficult, still in process:
I am trying to forgive myself
for bouts of inappropriate judgments,
meanness of spirit,
pettiness, envy, and unjust anger.
I am trying to forgive myself for not living up to my
   unreasonable expectations for myself.
I am trying to forgive myself
      for being human.

Yom Kippur is about forgiving other people as much as it is
about asking for forgiveness.

I wrote this before I was married and had a child. I'm sure the
specifics in this poem would be different at various stages of
my life.

Callus

The more I beat myself
the more I get callused.

The more I get callused
the more I get callous.

The more I get callous
the more I don't recall

that under this thick, shoe-leather skin,
is a soft,
juicy,
well-intentioned human heart.

Many people beat their chests during the *Yom Kippur* recitation
of communal sins.

God

I no longer think of God
as a man, looking a little like Ben Franklin,
a little like God in the Sistine Chapel,
his flowing white hair flying
in the howling grey wind,
frowning, looking down,
noting my every action,
keeping track of my every thought,
like an intrusive, judgmental parent.

I no longer see God
as part of a wispy cirrus cloud, blown by the wind into
    long streamers,
with his blank book and a Sharpie pen,
keeping score,
inscribing my destiny for the next year
at the end of *Yom Kippur*,
then slamming the book shut,
and sealing it.

Instead, I feel God
in the presence of congregants surrounding me
in the melody of familiar prayers
in the voice of the person *davening* next to me
in the sun angling through the window
in the sound of my own breath
        in the force that inspires me to grapple
            with the God images
        like moist clay, to remold them,
        because it's not the image that's God,
        it's the molding.

Warning: I wrote this poem when I was furious at God for not giving me what I thought I deserved.

Where I am This Year

Sitting.
Waiting.
But I left my heart at home this year.
I'm supposed to ask you to forgive me,
to pardon me,
to provide succor so I can choose right
right now
and from now on.
But you changed the rules on me, God,
or maybe I never truly understood the game,
and where I am this year
is wanting you
to apologize to me.

It was supposed to add up:
I'd be good
I'd do right
— with my heart, my head,
my words, my intentions —
I'd get what I deserved,
I'd be written in the Book.
Maybe that was naive.
Maybe I didn't get it
from the get-go.
Maybe I didn't want the responsibility.
Maybe I was afraid to grow up.
But once I moved beyond thinking of you
as the Old Man with the cotton-candy beard,
when I thought about you

and talked to you
I assumed you were the force
to combine science and math,
that you could sort the patterns of chaos
and mold them into shape,
that you were the One
who kept people from putting a period
at the end of Life is Unfair.

This year
I am an apple
that fell off the tree;
my skin intact,
my flesh, underneath, bruised brown.
Taste me: I'm bitter
and out of place,
like *Pesach*'s horseradish
when it's supposed to be new year's honey.

So where I am this year
is inside myself
trying to breathe
at least one sweet breath
into the emptiness.

And wherever I am this year
if I knock on my chest
where my heart lives
I won't be beating myself up.

My hand will make contact with my body
providing whatever warmth I can muster
because
I understand
it's my job
my place
my position
to puzzle all the pieces together
and they just may not add up.

What this all means
is where I am this year
is fallen
like an apple shaken prematurely from a tree.

Going Through the Motions

These are the motions of *Yom Kippur*:
Rising,
Sitting,
Bowing your obstinate head,
Rising on tiptoes to holy (three times),
Shifting your weight from side to side,
Rising,
Sitting,
Knocking on your chest where you used to
    pledge allegiance,
Doing it again and again,
Trying to stay awake,
Ignoring your headache, your avalanche hunger,
and the little devil voices that urge you to tune out,
Rising,
Sitting,
Moving your mouth at the same time as others,
and swallowing your stale saliva.

Sometimes,
there are times,
when meaning is elusive,
when reason is hiding around the corner,
when you know no one is listening,
that there's no book
to sign,
or seal,
that you just go through the motions
just because,
just to be part of something
to see if just doing it makes it yours.

Sometimes,
there are times,
when life feels unfair,
when there can't be any cosmic plan,
when you know there's no place for prayer to go
— except out the cracks of the windows,
or up to the ceiling like lingering smoke —
that you just go through the motions
— those every-year motions —
just because,
like learning to lift weights,
just to see if you can do it,
just because you're willing to commit for the
   long haul
in spite of the searing pain.

Sometimes, at these times,
when you don't know why,
you're lucky,
and you go through the motions
— a circus tiger jumping through its fiery hoop —
and out the other side,
and you find yourself
revived.

On the Day I Forgave God

On the day I forgave God
I went through my clothes closet,
tried on things I hadn't worn for a while
and made two piles: what to wear, what to give away.

I'd been meaning to do this for years
but was afraid to find out how much didn't fit,
so I held on to things, hoping I'd change back to
   who I was before
when everything was possible
and I didn't have to think too much.

But by holding on to what I'd had
I'd kept myself in limbo,
hoping to go backwards to fit into the past,
which kept me from moving forward.

I never thought,
"Silly, get rid of the old stuff and get new."
I was stuck there, hanging, for years.

Then, I got it,
that I'm bigger now, and older,
and take up more space in the world.

So I lost myself in my closet,
creating more space and emerging lighter,
shedding things that haven't felt right for a while.

Finally, I could reach the closet window,
opened it,
and the spirit of God drifted right
back in.

Yom Kippur Feast

Right around now
I start to crave something sweet
So I let my thoughts land
    like a honeybee lighting on clover
on things I did this year that I'm proud of,
or that show growth,
the fruits of my work,
and I am satisfied.

Right around now
I start to crave something salty
So I let my thoughts flow
    like tears that marked the calendar
over events that moved me
and I remember that the tears stopped,
but left tracks of humanity on my cheeks,
and I am satisfied.

Right around now
I start to crave something chewy
So I let my thoughts connect
    like a bite that doesn't need braces
on concepts I grappled with this year,
and I recall that I bit off small pieces
and chewed them into consciousness,
swallowed what I could accept,
and spit out what felt wrong,
and I am satisfied.

Right around now
I crave something thirst-quenching
So I let my thoughts separate
        like orange sections you give to distance runners
into what I did well, and where I fell short of my
    capabilities and heart
and what still remains, and what I can give up,

I forgive myself for being human.
I celebrate that I had a year, and there's another one
    ahead,
and I am satisfied.

Keeping the Gate Open

Honestly,
I used to imagine God,
who looked an awful lot like a gaunt Santa
wrapped in a Halloween sheet and
a thou-shalt-not scowl.
I used to imagine him
— always a him —
standing in a cotton-ball cloud
even on sunny, hot *Yom Kippurs*,
holding a hard-bound book
open in the middle,
looking like a mix of Charlton Heston and my
    grandfather Frankel,
peering down.
He had a pen in his hand
— a top-of-the-line Mont Blanc —
and was ready to write my name and address
on the "good" or "bad" list
in indelible ink,
— the kind my mother used for marking my sleep-
    away-camp clothes —
at the last minute
and that would be that for the year.
The gates — spiked iron, like those surrounding the
    mental hospital near where I grew up— would close
and I'd be stuck
with a good year to live up to
or a bad year to live down.

But what I did that year didn't really matter;
there was no cause-and-effect
because it had been preordained
by the ordained Big Man.

God looks a lot different these days;
now, a faceless puff of ungraspable cloud,
genderless,
glowing.

And I have my own book and pen,
that I use to make right and wrong.
I stand by the gate,
my foot stuck out like a doorstop
so the gate doesn't ever close,
so we can all go back and forth,
so we can all choose
all year long.

Looking Forward

I've always thought of *Yom Kippur* as an end,
the end of a year in which I, like all people strong
   enough to be honest,
made mistakes,
some big, some not so, some so tiny they can float
   away on a breath.

My own *Yom Kippur* prayers have always followed
   this structure:
I goofed,
I'm sorry,
I'll try to not do it again.

I've always rushed to repent before The Book of Life
— heavy and dusty —
slammed down hard on my fingers
while they were penciling in one more promise to
   not-do,
just one more.

For me, *Yom Kippur* has been about the past,
tying up loose ends that untied like kids' sneakers,
mopping up after myself, after crying
   unintended tears,
and patching the plaster of crumbling foundations.

Sorry-and-never-again is very glass-half-empty,
and these days I'm teaching myself to divine for water
   and fill that glass.

So thanks to something I read from
   Rabbi Schneerson,
the esteemed *Lubavitcher Rebbe,*
I'm trying something new this year:
I'm looking forward more than back.

Instead of thinking, *Last year I made a mistake*
— say, the mistake of being impatient —
this year I'll think, *I'm going to be patient.*

Instead of thinking, *Last year I goofed*
— let's say I judged people before knowing
   them well —
this year I'll think, *I'm going to be slow to judge,*
(*if, in fact, I judge at all.*)

So thank you, Rabbi Schneerson, and thank you,
   mistakes.
Thank you, water
and thank you, glass.
This year, after the fast,
I will fill you.

SUKKOT

Explanation of words, phrases, and concepts appearing in the Sukkot poems

SUKKOT, which begins five days after *Yom Kippur*, is named after the huts (*sukkot* in Hebrew) in which Jews are supposed to live during this week-long celebration. According to rabbinic tradition, these insubstantial sukkot represent the huts in which the Israelites lived during their 40 years of wandering in the desert after escaping from slavery in Egypt.

A **Sukkah** must consist of three walls and its roof made from objects that grow from the ground, such as branches or reeds. The roof must be wind-resistant and the sky must be visible from the inside. The interior of the *sukkah* is often decorated with seasonal fruits and vegetables, Judiac imagery, and children's artwork.

Coming in early autumn, *Sukkot* also celebrates the coming-to-fruition of many types of plants.

For **challah**, see *Rosh Hashanah* explanations.

An **etrog** is a citrus fruit, often thought to be the citron, used during *Sukkot*. Along with a **lulav** — a palm branch joined by myrtle and willow branches — it is held and waved during parts of the synagogue service. An *etrog* is usually wrapped well to prevent damage.

For **opening the door for Elijah**, see Passover explanations.

The **pitom** is the tip of an *etrog* that attaches it to the tree.

For **tzimmes**, see Hanukkah explanations.

***The **ushpizin** — literally, "visitors" — are the ancestors who are summoned into the sukkah to "enjoy" a meal.

Traditionally, Jewish patriarchs and matriarchs are invited, but it has become customary to include mention of one's own ancestors and other meaningful people.

The Weavers were an American folk music quartet, formed in 1948, that sang traditional folk songs from around the world, as well as blues, gospel, labor songs, children's music, and American ballads. They are regarded as the group that started the folk music revival in America. They were very politically progressive. **Pete Seeger**, The Weavers' banjo player, was not only a gifted musician and an early proponent of world music, but he also was an ardent social activist for a wide variety of causes throughout his life.

***Definition from the *Dictionary of Jewish Words*.
See **page xxv** for more information.

SUKKOT

Clearing a Path to God

In fall, it's easy:
You look up through the *sukkah* roof.

But at other times, you have to choose to clear a path
   to God.
You need strength,
arms, and legs, and a back, and breath.
You need the proper tools —
in summer, a scythe, a shovel in winter,
a pruner and shears for spring.

You need to believe in a path under the overgrown.
You need to know you may never get there.
But the trying, the clearing, the hacking away
means you've already arrived.

God as the Roof of Your Hut

The silvery-grey rain will come in
and the wind-whipped circles of leaves,

but God's fingers, twined like "Here is the Church,
Here is the Steeple,"
are a sieve, winnowing out the dross,
the dregs, and the chaff,
protecting you,
and preventing the shards of the Chicken-Little sky
    from falling down.

The gaps let in the stars
— the twinkly brooch on a great-aunt's chest —
and the moon shine
— the hooch that sings you to sleep —
and the blanket of black, with its satin edge,
that you tuck under your chin at night,

and the first sneaky glimpses of the glitter-orange
    morning.

The First Time I Prayed in Years

The squirrels
gnawed at the gourds and squashes
and crumbly corn-husk stalks
in the *sukkah*,
feasting on easy food,
not having to frantically find nuts as daylight waned.

They scurried away as I approached
but didn't go far,
posing frozen by the weather-faded construction-
    paper chains
and the rain-stained cornucopia drawings,
even their wispy tails stilled.

They waited for me to leave
so they could resume stoking up for trying times,
trusting in the bounty under an open sky,
trusting in their entitlement,
trusting that they would be provided for,

as I did,
for the first time in years.

Temporary Huts in the Wilderness

Don't fool yourself:
Even your stone Victorian, which has withstood the
    barrage of hundreds of seasons,
or your '50s split-level, or a ranch with a stucco face,
or the slice of a steel-gut high-rise you call your sweet
    home —
it's all temporary.
Buildings are mortal, too,
with expected life spans
and vulnerability to certain diseases
(as insurance tables will tell you.)
And although you can count on them
to shelter you from wet, and cold,
and provide you with somewhere to hang your hat,
and plug in your microwave,
and surrender every night,
homes get worn out, and down,
like the Adirondacks, which are so much shorter,
and so much older,
than the Rockies.

And even if you live in the electric nerve center of a
    throbbing, caffeinated city,
or a sidewalked burb where you presume to own land
    and lion-tame the lawn as proof,
or a farm where you play games of will and futility
    with your pig-headed piece of property,
it's still all the wilderness.

Even cement and asphalt,
and the tromp-tromping of life,
can't smother the earth, the ground underneath
which, like a cowlick, refuses to lie down and die.

No matter where, or how,
we all live in temporary huts
in the wilderness.

The Ushpizin: Seven Guests

There's not a door to open
like for Elijah, six months later,
(when the early-spring air comes in
and gently nudges the flame,
and the children, knowing Halloween, see ghosts.)

In fact,
roofless,
and gaping on one side,
the *sukkah* stands bare
before the elements that lick it, and beat it, and
  caress it,
    and the birds who haven't yet left,
    whose impulses urge them to swoop down
    and steal the silk that wraps the *etrog*,
    and the popcorn chains,
    to stash them for building next year's nests,
      and the emanations
      who drift in like foreshadowing autumn,
      who leave tooth marks on the gourds,
      and forget to collapse the folding chairs
  when they're gone.

Even with all these visitors
— a full house, like a jar jammed with air —
I want to send a two-stamp invitation
— engraved
on heavy paper,
calligraphy addressed —
to seven guests
to whom I'd serve my mother's *tzimmes*
and compote,
outside,

like the "who would you invite to a party" game,
alive or dead:
the uncle I never knew;
the woman who taught me, at middle age, to swim;
E.B. White, on the day he finished Charlotte's Web;
my fifth-grade teacher, Mrs. Demetri, who loved me;
the next-door-neighbor I loved;
Miriam;
and the egg lady.

But there isn't a door to open in the *sukkah*;
come, stand with me.
The *lulav* looks weary,
and birds have picked at the popcorn chains
leaving spaces like lost teeth.
Still,
I welcome you,
each for yourself
or all at once,
surrounding me like the silk around the *etrog*.
Let me feed you
and loan you a sweater
or a flannel shirt
and tell you that joining me outside in the *sukkah*
means you've already made your way
inside.

Turn, Turn, Turn

I'd like to ask Pete Seeger to supper in my *sukkah*.
He'd be a heavenly guest, one of my own quirky
  ushpizin.
I'd serve vegetable stew on brown rice
and a seedy home-made bread
and after a local, seasonal pie.
I'd turn to him, and tell him
how I grew up, and in, on his music,
how The Weavers was my family's soundtrack,
how my parents didn't care about the politics
but just liked the songs, and sang along
— and our family didn't sing much —
especially my father, in a buffalo-plaid shirt,
at an Adirondacks bungalow,
on the steps to a screened-in porch,
holding up the trout he'd caught on Schroon River
like a *Torah* just taken from the Ark.

After I'd served tea, and offered sweaters against the
  autumn night,
I'd turn to Pete, and tell him
how his songs, and the banjo,
and that beckoning voice of his youth,
are the best sounds of my innocent soul,
the part that's pure, that's remained unmarred;
that his songs blessed me with things to believe in,
and how, to this day, I'm not only willing,
but I'm desperate for him to raise a hand between
  strums,
and point to me, to us, urging us to sing together, to
  sing along,
to sing for God-knows-what something.

The *sukkah* rustles in the wind, leaves crackle,
weary season's-end mosquitos make a half-
    hearted appearance.
I wrap my father's buffalo-plaid shirt around me;
I wear some of his clothes now that he's gone.

Pete would turn to me, nod, then look away,
and sit up higher in his brittle, reedy body.
He'd hold up his hand as if to part waters
and point,
and every person sitting in any *sukkah*
anywhere in the world at that moment
would start singing that song from Ecclesiastes,
the one about time for this, and time for that,
and the four-part harmony would rise out of
    the *sukkahs*
towards heaven, if there is one,
like sweet, good-hearted smoke.

Many thanks to *Jewish Currents*, which originally published
this poem.

Harvest

It is the beginning
of leaving,
of falling,
of one more attempt at stripping off the green,
when the night-blooming cereus blooms by the
   fullmoonlight,
an orange-metal glow,
with reticent blossoms
— jagged pink and the white of spirit —
which, after waiting,
at just the right time,
— on a night when no one should be alone —
expand into two sweet fruit,
citrus nipples intact like a commandment,
flowing unwatched onto the cheeks
of uncertain September air,
in the rain,
and the earth opens up in acceptance.

Three branches rustle in sympathy
in the quiet of the remaining cicadas.
The creek rushes toward its destination.
Apples blush,
and the desire of the tomatoes
is to be picked
in the field
by the tracks.
The next morning,
after all the leaves have fallen,
what's left
is a skeleton,
like the roof of a tenacious barn,

an open hut to the rain,
all hung with fruit that hasn't fallen
yet.

Sukkot Woman

Four friends about to bear fruit
at harvest time,
settling in for the winter,
snuggling, suckling,
amber warmth glowing the hearth,
the barn already full.

The childless woman watches
at harvest time,
wishing to gather fruit
unbearable heart tick-ticking, empty,
years of months have passed.

Under the edgeless full-fire moon
she becomes an apple tree,
her feet planted, roots mingle.
A bird rushes in, lands softly,
rustles, its head under its wing.
And an apple falls.

There are many types of apples.
There are many ways to bear fruit.

Etrog I

What looks like a hand grenade,
smells like baby wipes
and, if we could hear it,
would sound like early Beach Boys?

What looks like a cartoon breast with a perfect nipple,
smells like Pledge
and, if we could drink it,
would taste like sidewalk-sale lemonade?

What looks like sunrise
— if morning could bear fruit —
smells like squeaky adolescent cologne
and, if we held it,
would feel like oblong earth, bumpy and ridged?

Etrog II

I didn't know
there was an English word
for *etrog*.
Etrog was etrog, and that was that.

I didn't know
that *etrog* was a "citron"
(which sounds like the fancy French car.)

I didn't know
it has more spice and sweet than a lemon,
its rind familiar to fruitcake
(which is far less welcome than guests at my *sukkah*.)

The Pitom

It's like virginity
of a bride
just a generation or two back:
To matter,
the *pitom* has to be intact.

It's the umbilical cord knot,
the part that shows,
and reveals the fruit's connection
to the source that fed it,
and from which it has been plucked.

The *pitom* matters
— not because we fear imperfection
or from some manifest fussiness —
but because a *pitom*, intact,
reveals the perfect time for harvesting,
when what grows leaves home
at the exact, precise moment:
Not too soon,
when the wrenching would have broken off the *pitom*,
and not too late,
by which time the *etrog* would have twisted itself free
and fallen from the tree to the ground.
The *pitom*, in place, speaks of balance,
like a wishbone that breaks in half
cleanly, and right in the middle,
and everybody wins.

It is time to harvest;
it is time to reap.

The *pitom*
isn't about fretting our bungling fingers
or shushing the clumsy curiosity of children,
as it is about tuning in
to how there's a perfect time
and a precise moment
to the fall, and falling apart,
in the order of things.

Hurricane

The carnivorous season's-end hurricane
tore trees limb by limb,
dislocated branches from their sockets,
then licked the sap like a lion's bloody paw.

When it was over,
we gathered the displaced twigs and switches for our
  sukkah
— their shocked, sear leaves contorted —
and they strained to embrace us with their raggedy,
  angular arms,
their jagged legs, unsteady.

And at the end of the last day,
we shook the three most crippled boughs
— all turning the brown of dying —
and, to the scent of citrus, fire and fall,
released them to the wind.

What Do You Do With an Etrog

when *Sukkot* gives way to *Simhat Torah*?
Don't eat it, or compost it, authorities warn;
etrogs are full of pesticides.
They are delicate, unlike their in-your-nose Lemon
   Pledge smell,
and spoil even if you just rub one against another on
   the branch.
An *etrog* that makes the cut for *Sukkot*
has to be blemish-free,
like the girl who gets voted prom queen.

Think of all the hands that have held it
and shaken it, and passed it on to other hands.
Think especially of the kids, those nose-drippy
   Hebrew-school kids,
who sniff against the *etrog*,
and with fingers,
explore its lumps like a topographic map
        during an *etrog's* eight days of glory,
             the eight days that give its life meaning,
             the eight days when we ask it to stand in
                for a heart.

But because we are cautioned not to eat an *etrog*,
it's easy to forget that it's just a fruit,
that it grows on an *etrog* tree
  — an evergreen, like belief —
that the tree has thorns
and a lifespan.

At the end of *Sukkot,*
thank the *etrog* for being yellow.
Thank it for being bumpy, and redolent of something
  you can't quite name.
Thank it for doing what it intended.
and then,
let the *etrog* be
and then, let it go.

SHEMINI ATZERET

*Explanation of words, phrases, and concepts
appearing in the*
Shemini Atzeret poem

***SHEMINI ATZERET, celebrated on the seventh day of *Sukkot*, marks the conclusion of the fall harvest festival. Special ancient prayers thank God for the harvest and ask for winter rain to prepare the ground for spring planting.

These additional prayers last until Passover.

***Definition from the *Dictionary of Jewish Words*.
See **page xxv** for more information.

A Shemini Atzeret Prayer for Rain, 2017

"No more water, fire next time"

In this autumn of killer hurricanes and earthquakes,
acres and acres of California are charring black,
muddy, molten, melted,
flat, and barren.
The burning fires turn the blue sky a ghastly orange,
the wind, sooty, so thick it catches in your throat,
its stink sticking to hair, clothing, and curtains
    blowing in open windows.

Everything is tinder:
An ancestor's maple chiffonier,
a new leather coat, tags still on,
photos of the wedding,
the cat's collar, the dog's leash,
the hose, the trowel, the shovel, the weed-whacker,
the just-graduated-from tricycle,
yesterday's groceries, with food for tomorrow's party,
the sycamores out front, the lilac bush, and tithonia,
all the jewelry,
the soccer trophies, cleats, and shin guards,
the autographed copy of "Charlotte's Web" with its
    original dust jacket,
all
the
other
books,
the beds,
the scented candles,
the large carton of Charmin from Sam's Club,

the suitcase of love letters, locked,
the Subaru with 135,439 miles.

Gone.

Leaving ash, cinders,
and more.
Gone.
Leaving shards of stuff that trick you and make you
   think they're still attached to something intact,
gone in a flash,
leaving a dull shock,
a flash of ravenous fire that blows through and
   doesn't lose its breath.

How can you think this fire isn't the beginning
of the end?

Prayers for rain for agricultural concerns are said at services
starting on *Shemini Atzeret* — the last day of *Sukkot* — through
Passover. But because of huge and destructive fires as a result
of climate change, we now have to pray for rain to survive.

SIMCHAT TORAH

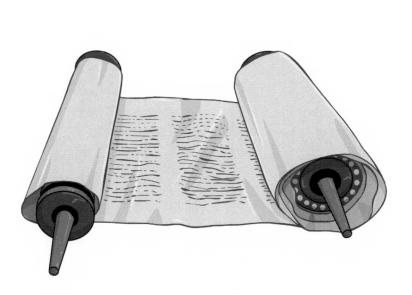

Explanation of words, phrases, and concepts appearing in the Simchat Torah poems

SIMCHAT TORAH celebrates the completion of the annual cycle of reading the *Torah*, also called The Five Books of the Hebrew bible. Traditionally, people dance with the *Torah* and generally make merry.

At *Simchat Torah* services, some synagogues unwind the *Torah* by having congregants standing in a large circle and holding it, and then rewinding the scroll back to the beginning.

Even in synagogues where women are forbidden to touch, hold, or read from the *Torah*, *Simchat Torah* offers a welcome, joyous break from that prohibition. (Happily, there are many congregations where women have an unrestricted relationship with the *Torah* throughout the year.)

***The **ark** is the cabinet at the front of the synagogue that houses the *Torah* scrolls. It is usually set into or against a wall that faces East toward Jerusalem. A depiction of the Ten Commandments is usually part of its design.

***Bereshit** is the name of the book of Genesis, the first book of the *Torah*.

Some people think that **re-reading the *Torah***, year after year, would be repetitive, and that after a few times through all five books that there's nothing much more to learn. Not true.

***Definition from the *Dictionary of Jewish Words*.
See **page xxv** for more information.

Bereshit: And It Was Good

In the beginning
there was an empty book:
Its paper, skins of wildness,
its cover, a lattice of sticks
tied with cornsilk, guts, and strips of fronds.

In the beginning
there was a forever well of ink:
Its color, chameleon,
its texture, goat's milk
that flowed as if a heartbeat.

In the beginning
there was a Some-being:
Its voice, resonant and echo-y,
its imagination, a sunrise fireball
that burns, but never out.

And sometime after the beginning
the Some-being who had created these things
created light: splinters of glass, and prisms,

and with the ink on the paper, the book began to
  be written,
and with the eyes of the newborn, the book began to
  be read.

To The Rabbi at The Ark
Taking out The Torah

For Rabbi Elliot Holin

You are a midwife.
You open the doors of the Ark
and out rush the birth waters
that surround us like the warm embrace
of the ocean in late August.
You reach inside, skilled with practice,
and bring forth the baby
who, miraculously, is already swaddled in silk,
and belted in linen sewn with signs of the zodiac.
Then, like Mufasa showing off Simba at cliff's edge,
you lift it for everyone to admire,
long enough for people to notice
that what you're holding glows like diamonds
and a sea of molten silver,
the words inside of gold.

The Torah as Milk

It's the food of source, the first food,
the best, as if from the breasts
of women, it nourishes like nothing else,
its purpose to feed, to fill
the need that howls when empty,
a beast, a primitive need for succor,
to suckle, for filling,
fulfilling the cry for full
that growls otherwise and cries
at all hours and keeps awake yowling
because it wants, the soothing,
the whole, the whiteness,
the completion.

Holding the Torah

It's like holding a baby who's getting too big to be held:
You still want to snuggle it close, even though it's
    heavy and loose-limbed,
and its weight staggers, forcing you to focus on
    your balance.

You're a little self-conscious, and imagine, correctly,
    that everyone is
        watching
as you struggle with it, awkward, hoping it won't
    come undone
in a heap of parchment with perfect black marks,
    its tale.

You want to keep and contain it, and smell its wisdom,
and stroke its velvet coat like a beloved teddy bear
— even dance with it like a partner who knows
    your steps,
        your breath, your heft, how to intertwine —
but as soon as you think you may have found
    the knack
you have to pass it on to the next person with a
    dance card.

But your arms will understand, and remember.

The First Time I Danced with the Torah
(as a freshman at Boston University)

I remember
taking to the streets
with the *Torah* and a crowd, dancing
— not like Astaire or Fosse —
but with a fever, a fervor
from following the law to the letter
on an open promenade
named for Martin Luther King

and dancing, a conga line, a snake,
a wedding crush, singing, too
and I got to hold it for a while
it was bulky and held me back like a clumsy partner
I felt its weight like a burden, and yet a beloved
and who cared who was watching

that night, it was *Simchat Torah*
and I was one of many mouths
and legs and arms encircling, enveloping
creating energy that rose and fell
back down upon us like a light rain and yes,
no, it has never happened like that since.

The Woman Holds the Torah, and Wishes to Dance

Some people believe
I shouldn't touch, or embrace, even,
this perfect scroll today,
as it's unrolled back
to its beginnings
or even, that my woman's touch, or even
breath, insults, and tarnishes it

and the reason, they whisper,
if asked, is that it's too heavy,
and cumbersome,
    Have you ever carried a flailing five-year-old?
and it'll fall, or make me topple
in its awkwardness, and touch
the ground, unholy

and I say, this book is about the ground,
about being planted, firm, and sprouting
unevenly upward,
and that it's earth, not dirt,
and that mud cools stings
and makes bricks,

and I say, look at these arms,
that carry, and calm, that child you've disquieted,
who I'm used to balancing
like a waitress, and have never fallen
so far that I can't get up,
and that what you see as contagion
I offer as my strength, and if you'll just step away,
I'll show you how I can
carry, and dance.

Unwinding the Book

As the year unfurls like a new flag before the wind
we unwind the Book
week by week, twist by twist, bit by bit,
the balance shifts from left to right
as the scrolls wait for us to eavesdrop on their tales,
stories with shape, images of substance.
Like a roll of film grabbing life frame by frame
it uncoils, and what's small becomes bigger
while what's large loses matter like the Milky Way,
and just when you think you're steady
it's a new week,
and last week's equilibrium
doesn't work.

Starting Over

There's no such thing as going
back to the beginning without
bringing with you what you've
learned since. You can't
return to your hometown without
carrying all the cities you've
subsequently seen. You can't reconnect
with your former beloved without
lugging along those you loved in between. You
can't eat this season's first melon
without last year's fruit in your
mouth's memory. There's only a first
time once; it's poignant to have had, or done,
even if it's all been good. But to go
back to the Books each year, to
start over and layer now upon
a foundation of already, is a delight.
What's passed makes the present more
rich, its textures more intricate, its
tastes multi-tiered. It may be the same
soup, but this mix of seasonings has never been.

HANUKKAH

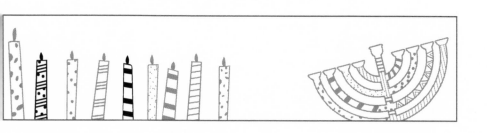

Explanation of words, phrases, and concepts appearing in the Hanukkah poems

HANUKKAH is a joyous eight-day holiday about a military victory and what is considered the Hanukkah miracle. The Maccabees were the band of Jewish revolutionaries, led by Judah Maccabee, who fought for religious freedom and the right to reclaim Jerusalem from King Antiochus and Syrian control. After winning back the Second Temple, the Jews found it had been desecrated with statues of Greek Gods, so they needed to clear and rededicate it. Also, there was only one-day's worth of a special oil to light the *ner tamid*, or eternal flame, but it lasted for eight days, which is thought to be miraculous.

***The **bimah** is the raised platform or stage from which the Torah is read and services are led.

For **blintzes,** see **Shavuot** explanations.

Bubbe is the Yiddish word for grandmother.

***A **bubbe meise**, literally a "grandmother's story," is used to describe a superstitious story or "old wives' tale."

Bar mitzvah boys and girls used to get pelted with **candy,** thrown by the congregation, after finishing their *Torah* portion, supposedly to demonstrate the sweetness of the occasion and of *Torah* study. Happily, this tradition seems on the way out, or softer candies are provided to the congregation.

The constellation **Cassiopeia** is the Lady in the Chair.

For **door opened to welcome the Prophet Elijah,** see Passover explanations.

***A dreidel is a four-sided spinning top used in a game during Hanukkah. Each *dreidel* has a Hebrew letter on each side — nun, gimmel, hay, and shin — which together stand for a phrase that means "a great miracle happened there [Israel]." To play the *dreidel* game, everyone starts with the same number of gelt pieces. When you spin a *nun*, nothing happens. When you spin a *hay*, you win half of the "pot" or "kitty." When you spin a *shin*, you put one piece of *gelt* in the "kitty." When you spin a *gimmel*, you win the entire "kitty."

Gelt is a foil-wrapped chocolate coin, the typical currency used in playing *dreidel*.

Hanukkah always falls on or near the Northern Hemisphere's winter solstice, the shortest day in the year.

Hineni means "Here I am," and is mostly used when God personally calls on someone in the Bible to do something difficult and important.

The King of Ninevah, Nebuchadnezzer, sends his general, Holofernes, to subdue his enemies, the Jews. **Judith,** a beautiful widow, sneaks into the enemy camp, gets Holofernes drunk, and cuts off his head.

Latkes are fried potato pancakes made to celebrate Hanukkah.

Machetunim is a Yiddish word that refers to one's extended family by marriage, and especially the in-laws.

For **matzah,** see Passover explanations.

A **matzah brei**, also called fried *matzah*, is a combination of water-softened *matzah* and eggs, which is fried.

A **menorah** is an eight-branched candleholder used at Hanukkah. It is sometimes called a *hanukkiah*.

For **Nahshon,** see Passover explanations.

For *Pesach,* see Passover explanations.

A *shamash* is the ninth candle on the *menorah*, used to light the other candles.

Ta'am is a Hebrew word that means, literally, flavor — usually in a positive way.

A *tzimmes* is a baked dish of vegetables or fruit.

Kasha varnishkes are cooked buckwheat groats combined with cooked bowtie noodles.

A *Yiddische kop* means having the mental agility for traditional Jewish scholarship, or simple common sense.

***Definition from the *Dictionary of Jewish Words*.
See **page xxv** for more information.

Apples and Sneakers

It's like comparing apples to sneakers
or oranges to bookcases:
Hanukkah and Christmas just don't balance
  each other.
They don't even get weighed on the same scale
or use the same computation
to determine their worth
(as meaningless as comparing miles to ounces.)
Impossible.
Immeasurable.
Like choosing which of your children you love best.

If they were boxers, they wouldn't be allowed in the
  same ring:
Christmas is a heavyweight,
Hanukkah, light.

But to keep us from feeling deprived
      especially our kids, who are attracted to the
          blinking lights,
      and the red-and-green,
      and the warm, cozy blanket of Christmas,
we've appropriated Christian customs
and created false equivalents.
We send each other Hanukkah cards,
decorate a Hanukkah bush,
display a "seasonal" wreath,
sing "holiday" carols (even if we don't say "Christ"
  out loud,)
buy our kids eight days of Hanukkah presents
so they, too, have the latest-craze toys.

There are two things we have to figure out:
How to make what we offer
memorable and sweet
and filled with rituals with staying power,
even if our richest holy days came months earlier;

and how to let go of feeling inferior,
that what we offer can't even compete,
so we don't worry
that Christmas will swoop down on our children
like a reindeer who's lost his sense of direction
and steal them away in a sleigh headed north.

What Hanukkah is About

Ask a group of children
        who are devouring *latkes*
        with applesauce and sour cream
        and opening this-year's-latest glittery gifts
        from Toys-R-Us
        and unwrapping gold-covered chocolate coins
        that drain the *dreidel* "kitty"
what Hanukkah is about
and they'll tell you the *bubbe meise*
about the oil
and the eight days of light
and "the great miracle that happened" there.

If they mention the Maccabees at all
it'll be to talk about rededicating the Temple
        which they don't really "get,"
        since we don't have one spiritual
                center anymore
        and maybe what they imagine
        is a freshly scrubbed altar and *bimah*
        that smell, for a few days, of lingering Lysol
and not the years of blood
with the Greeks
and the Jews who'd wrapped themselves in
    Greek-like ways.

And if you tell them more about the Maccabees
unless you draw pictures
even with a palette of words
they won't imagine the viscera of war
        like a sausage split open
        at battle sites,

and the smell of rot
that makes you retch your insides out
but rather,
some military parade
with decorated men
forming straight lines
and moving as if one.

And although they'll learn
some day
that you sometimes have to fight
with words or weapons
for the right thing,
and although you probably want them
to know the truth
all the truths
the whole story
so they can decide on their own
about how to turn wrong around,

it's nice
for now, at least,
for the children
while they're young
and still believe
that God really keeps score in a big book of life,
and Elijah (our slightly Santa counterpart)
may someday show up for dinner when we
open the door

not to focus on the Maccabees
and their military high-and-mighty

and snake-like political maneuvers
    but to be open to
    and maybe help create
    another way of change
    that can't be forced
    but can be nurtured
    and encouraged
    and a stage set for its appearance:
A miracle.

Cheese

Being a smart cookie with a *Yiddishe kop*,
Judith invited the invader to dinner
and prepared a feast
that would, in restaurant-kitsch,
be called a "groaning board,"
with a parade of dish after dish
— like you'd see, animated,
to music, in a Disney movie —
the type of spread you put together
when you've invited over
your prospective *machetunim*,
and you want to impress them
with your ethnic savoir-faire
— a real over-the-top,
pull-out-all-the-stops type of affair —

but what made it most memorable
was that each item featured cheese —
salty, thirst-inducing cheese.
She melted Limberger on her *latkes*
and covered her ricotta-filled *blintzes*
with a coat of Muenster.
She sprinkled Pecorino on her *tzimmes*
and grated Gouda into her *matzah brei*.
She sliced chunks of Gorgonzola
in her *kasha varnishkes*
(and, just for secular slumming, there was Velveeta
in the macaroni and cheese.)
Dessert was sliced pears with Stilton
and a chaser of Cheshire,
as a fitting conclusion
to a feast that began with baked Brie.

To drink, she gave him wine,
Concord grape, room temperature,
left over from *Pesach.*
She asked him questions,
laughed at his jokes,
listened to his stories,
nodded "uh-huh,"
made eye contact,
asked for more
to keep him talking,
his mouth open,
to yack and drink
and drink and yack.

She turned his hairy, hoary head with attention
and then, when he was gone beyond drunk,
she lopped it off with the carving knife
she'd usually use
to slice the chicken.

So much for the invasion.

It all comes down to this:
When you want to win a war
or prevail in a battle
don't rely on weapons,
don't count on cunning:
Choose cheese.

What Does It Mean
to Defile a Holy Place?

It's more than not
sweeping the floors
or dusting the decorations.
It's more than not
vacuuming the rugs
or Windex-ing windows.

It's more than not keeping up;
it's about breaking down.

It's conscious and willful
    like a mustache graffiti,
    like a spraypainted swastika on a
       synagogue wall,
    like rape
knowing the spirit of the place
and choosing to steal it
and replace it,
deface it.

There are many types of holy places:
A room, a heart,
a conversation, a country.

We should each think of our self
as, at best, a holy place,
and guard our spirit
    — the one with the secret recipe, like Coke,
    the one we vowed at *Yom Kippur* —
against burglars and swindlers,
con men,

and too-good promise-makers,
 willfully,
 consciously,
 conscientiously,
knowing that dust is an everyday event,
knowing that dirt is everywhere,
knowing that
in all holy places,
keeping up
is the key to keeping out.

The Menorah

When the neighborhood was Jewish
and our block smelled like Hanukkah
— of soup, citrus, wax, horseradish —
my parents never put a *menorah* at the window
facing the street
even though you're supposed to
because we were afraid
the flames would catch the curtains on fire;
     because we didn't have, and felt superior,
     to an electric *menorah* with its too-orange
         fire-shaped bulbs;
and because we didn't need to:
Everyone who would see our window was like us
— Jewish and comfortable in it,
or not Jewish but comfortable in it —
     so we didn't need to advertise
     or make a statement
     or stand up against.

Traditionally,
if you're in danger
of being attacked by non-Jews
— in history, in Israel, on your block, in your head —
you're allowed to keep your *menorah* inside
on a table
in a room
so you can fulfill your obligation
to burn and melt
     without drawing attention to yourself
     without shouting *Hineni, Here I Am,*
     without being a stick which, if rubbed with
         another, could ignite a blaze.

But in the decades since,
since the exodus of us
    to Florida, to upscale suburbs,
    to divorce, or death,
and the influx of others
who don't really get it
that Hanukkah is not our Christmas,
    my parents bought an electric *menorah*
    — a plain one, without gewgaws, nonetheless —
which they display
and keep on through the night,
even with those too-orange fire-shaped bulbs,

as if to say there's another way
to respond to the threat of an attack
    even if that attack is a drip-by-drip wearing away
    instead of all at once;
even if that attack gnaws at identity
rather than the body;
    even if that attack isn't intentional or
        bad-spirited
    and not an attack, really,
but change.

Ta'am

The problem with *latkes*
is that they're best
when they're bad for you,
fried full of oil that's soaked in
    like water to parched desert soil
and if you blot them with a paper towel
before eating
the towel looks as oily
as the impression of your adolescent face
on a tissue.

One year, we baked them.
They had no *ta'am*.

And then there's the sour cream,
sybaritic little mounds of which
lounge alongside the latkes
like babes at a pool
inviting you in for a dip.
    But you don't eat sour cream any more
    — doctors' admonitions, nutritionists' advice —
    except when you accidentally forget
    to tell the waitress to leave it behind
    with your baked potato (and the butter.)
Thick, rich sour cream makes your mouth remember
your old-country *bubbe* and her high-fat kitchen.

One year, we used non-fat yogurt.
It had no *ta'am*.

And then there's the Hanukkah *gelt*,
those gold-covered chocolate coins

that you buy, ostensibly, for the kids to use
to play *dreidel* with their cousins and lady luck,
but you prefer, if truth be known,
Godiva and her high-class ways.
The candy is supposed to be a symbol,
to sweeten *Torah* study
— like being pelted at your bar mitzvah —
    but you know it's a high-fat,
    high-sugar,
    caffeinated source
    of what they call "empty calories"
    that'll buzz you up, and drop you harder,
    than your high-school sweetheart.

One year, we found carob coins in the health
   food store.
They had no *ta'am.*

So why is it
that Hanukkah's edible traditions
are bad for the heart
    and their healthful rivals so bland
that we let ourselves go
in spite of knowing better?

The answer is simple:
It would be easy to overlook Hanukkah
not only because of its proximity to Christmas
but because it's a holiday
    if we focus on the Maccabees and their
        military might
that could be heart-less.

It's a reminder to keep the heart in Hanukkah
and to focus on the miracle of candles,
and the reflections of light
    both of which, if edible,
      would have great *ta'am*.

The Miracle

The truth is,
there wasn't anything special
about the oil, or magic,
or unusual, or blessed, even,
about what the bottle held.

The only thing different
was that they wanted it to work
and, having done their own work
— the work of getting ready,
of reclaiming, of clearing out —
they were ready to receive,
even a miracle.
They held on tight to the farthest edges of wanting
— the ones that border on belief —
and started the fire with what they had.
Trust in one, they told themselves,
and that will be enough.
But because they were satisfied,
because it truly would have been enough,
one stretched into more,
and expanded into eight.

The truth is,
because they were ready,
they could have started the fire
from their own eager breath
and, being their own bellows,
could have kept it going
on and on
and on.

Bubbe's Menorah I

I never scrape off the melted wax
on my mother's mother's *menorah*.
I like the layers of color
and the textures of time
and underneath, the tarnish of greying age.

My mother, when she visits,
picks it off with her varnished fingernails
and the probing tines of a fork,
then polishes the *menorah* with a thick pink polish,
to a sparkle that again reflects flame.

Bubbe's Menorah II

For the first time since my parents died
I used the family *menorah*.
Made of a non-precious metal with limited shine,
it's nothing fancy:
> A row of tiny goblets to hold the candles
> and behind, two lions with menacing faces,
> — their heads too large for their bodies —
> turning away from each other.
> Above them, a Jewish star,
> topped by a tiny goblet for the *shamash*.

This *menorah* has a deadly design flaw:
Because the daily candles sit directly under
  the *shamash*,
The One That Lights The Others always melts
  too quickly
> bowing forward, sometimes, like a prayer,
> and ending in a final wisp of air
> that curls upward and gone
> while the other candles are still alive.

It must be hard for a candle
— if a candle has a soul —
to live out its time, even as it lessens,
> when the one who gave it life
> and lit the way
> is gone.

Shamash:
The One that Lights the Others

The one that lights the others
leads them out from darkness.
It must be fully on fire itself, first,
before performing its feat of illumination.
It has to stand tall
and withstand the fire from below, and next to,
    by not wilting, but waiting
    to be certain that all the others have caught on.
The *shamash* is the ice breaker,
the first to start a conversation,
the one to ask for a dance
    like *Nahshon* of the first step.
The *shamash* is the grunt,
the blue-collar worker,
the one who builds the foundation,
the one who makes the rest possible.

As we stand by the light of the *menorah*,
let us thank each *shamash* in our life
    who has freed us to shine,
and let us aspire, each, to be a *shamash*,
and enable others to reveal their light
and glow.

Women, Too

It is said
that the women, too,
are obliged to light the Hanukkah candles.
This is unusual;
in most cases, it's only the men who are obliged to
   do anything.

It's the women, usually,
who keep the home fires burning
from which the men kindle torches
to chase fear from the night.

It's the women, usually,
who play the role of pilot light
that are always on, on low,
but can burst into tall peaks of flame
on demand.

It's the women, usually,
who only feed the fires
as the men get credited
for the conflagration.

But at Hanukkah
it's not enough
for the women to feed, or nurture,
or stay in a steady state of readiness
like kept women.

At Hanukkah
it is said
for eight days

the women are required to act,
to take a symbolic stand,
to stand by the candles
and illumine them
    in hopes that the candles
    will stand by the women
    and shed light on who they can be,
    and illumine them
    in return.

While the Candles Burn

You're not supposed to work
while the candles burn.
You're not supposed to work
while the candles devour themselves
and transform themselves
     from substance to spirit
     from matter to light
     from wax to air
     from something you can hold
to something you only recall, and feel.

You're not supposed to work
while the candles burn.
You're not supposed to read by their light
or write by it.
You're not supposed to check off your December
  "to do" list
or address holiday cards
or compute year-end tax deductions
while the candles burn.

You're not supposed to use these candles
to light each other;
they're not supposed to perform
any function
except to eat themselves up
and, as they're doing that magic
     of disappearing while, at the same time,
     becoming something else
they're meant to slow you down
and force you to focus
and make you aware of a miracle.

Hanukkah brings with it
eight days of partial Shabbat
that last at least
a half hour
while the candles burn.

Miracles happen all the time
but if we've forgotten how to see them
if we've lost the skill of looking
    and seeing
    and receiving
    and being satisfied
then even fire
    with its red-and-gold-and-blue triangles
    and thin, black streak of soot ascending
will go unnoticed,
and our own chances for transformation
will have gone up in smoke
even as the candles burn.

Playing Dreidel

If you want to grow flowers
you need seeds
from flowers that have already been.

There has to be sourdough starter
before you bake bread
then break it.

And you can't play *dreidel*
unless you've put into the "pot."
You can't even start
until everyone has fed the "kitty,"
taken some of what they have
and giving it away
hoping to get more.
You need to give
to play
to win.

That's why rolling *shin*
is the holy roll
Rolling *shin* means you have to put in
to feed the hungry kitty
(who follows you around, mewing,
and hops in your lap if she's hungry.)
Rolling *shin* means you're keeping things going,
helping to continue the game,
contributing so things last beyond your turn.
You become oil, enough for just one day,
and give of yourself,
hoping,
and trusting

that others will give, too,
to feed the flame
to keep the game going.

Nun is boredom;
the game continues, but nothing changes.
Hay is greed;
you get half, which only makes you want more.
Gimmel is foreboding;
big winnings tease that there's an end to the game.
But it's the *shin*
— which looks like loss,
but is, really, the win,
the opportunity to keep the Game going —
that spells out, by itself, a great miracle happening,
and happening here.

Four Sides of the Dreidel:
Nun, Hay, Shin, Gimmel

When nothing happens, you're safe — but stuck with
   chocolate coins that maybe got stale.
When you claim half, you're happy — but unsatisfied
   because the rest coulda shoulda been yours.
When you put one in, you're forced to feel equal —
   but anxious to see who still has more.
When you win it all, you're ecstatic — but you fear
   losing it.

And if you feel guilty about the guy who goes broke,
   you deserve the *gelt*.

Light

Hanukkah descends
right on the edges
of the year's shortest day:
When darkness dominates
and hangs heavy
like a clothesline towel surprised by a storm,
when it's possible to spend a day
never being nuzzled by the peachy cheeks of sunlight,
when every day leading up to
has been about fading and losing and giving over,
without choice,
to giving up.

So we kindle the Hanukkah candles
and, in that, tell ourselves
that we're allowed
    to grapple
with the oozy shapes of darkness
which, when grasped, squoosh out of your fists;
    to fight,
maybe to win,
    to poke holes in a black-blanket sky,
through which we can see illumination,
and splotches of radiance

just as the stars emerge
and dot the sky like scattered rhinestones
which, if you link — like a child's connect-the-dots —
form outlines
like the Dipper, or Dog,
or even the Lady in the Chair
which you can grab, like rope,

162

to climb out of the darkness
and onto the other side;

just as the days about face
and elongate like a Modigliani,
and you've teetered eight days on the mountaintop,
long enough,
and can start down,
the other side,
and the days seem to get longer,
and lighter,
quicker than they took toward longer nights;

and you realize, once again,
that it was good to have lit your own candles
to know you can cope, if not change,
with the darkness,
and you'd know, if you'd just sat tight and waited,
rocking like the mother with her newborn,
that the other side, light,
would peek around the edges of the solstice
and take its place.

TU B'SHEVAT

Explanation of words, phrases, and concepts appearing in the Tu b'Shevat poems

TU B'SHAVET, the "birthday" of all fruit trees, is a minor festival. In ancient times, *Tu b'Shevat* was merely a date on the calendar that helped Jewish farmers establish exactly when they should bring their fruit from recently planted trees to the Temple as fruit offerings. Today, some people have a *Tu b'Shevat* seder, a festive meal featuring fruits in honor of the holiday.

Pear Tree

Outside, visible from our kitchen window,
was a pear tree. It was already there
when we moved in; my newly suburban parents
— survivors of grass pushing through
   pavement cracks,
and stickball on an asphalt schoolyard —
wouldn't have had the leap of imagination,
the vision of possibility,
to think of planting something as big and permanent
   as a tree,
let alone a tree that would provide fruit.

It was small, never reaching the roof of our one-
   story house,
and slim, easily overlooked.
Its branches were toned and lean, almost muscular;
its color muted, between green and grey.
My father never pruned or watered it,
yet that tree
— as determined as someone running away
   from something
and toward something else —
stubbornly produced seven or eight pears
year after year,
small, hard, and all but tasteless.

Every year, my father bit into the first pear
expectantly, as if judging a 4-H contest,
and pronounced it the best ever.
He then presented it to my mother, with the rest of
   the harvest,
and asked her to cook them up
to make compote.

My mother hated that damn tree
and its tough little pears
that never really softened
no matter how many hours they cooked in sugar water.
The tree, right outside the kitchen window,
watched the pears boil
and snickered at my well-intentioned mother
and the futility of her task.

But my father was committed to eating those pears.
So every year, she made that obstinate compote
to please him, to help him feel
— just two generations from the *shtetl* —
a little like a gentleman farmer
reaping this year's bounty.

Every year, he ate that compote
chewing, grinding each hard little mouthful,
and offered to share it with the rest of us.
We disappointed him by declining.

My parents are gone.
The house belongs to someone else
who added a second story,
and I live in another city.
I don't know if the tree still stands.

If it does, I believe
it still produces its crop, however limited,
of determined little fruit
that think enough of their own sweetness
to offer themselves as food.

How to Plant a Tree (for Tu b'Shevat)

(Directions for reading aloud: Lines in *italics* should be read in a strong, straightforward voice. Lines in regular type should be read with emotion. Can be read as call-and-response.)

Dig a wide hole, two or three times the width of the
   root ball.
Be optimistic.
Assume it will take, and flourish.
Things usually thrive if you give them enough space
and believe in their potential.
      So do people.

Place the tree; turn it so the best side of the tree is facing
   the direction you want.
Make sure it gets enough sun.
Assume it will absorb what it needs.
Things usually grow if you point them towards a
   source of nurture
and if you show them how to receive it, and
   encourage them along.
      So do people.

Backfill the hole, lightly packing the soil as you go.
Don't pack down the soil, hard, with the back of
   your shovel.
Assume it needs to be loose so there are openings for
   the new roots to explore.
Things usually fill the space they're given
and will wilt, even die, without enough.
      So do people.

Stake the tree
Drive the stake through the root ball into the
    ground underneath.
Assume the tree wants to take hold.
Things want to stand up straight
And will do so if, at the bottom, they're secure.
        So do people.

*Tip: Newly planted trees should only be pruned to remove
    broken, dead, or diseased limbs. Otherwise, leave them
    until after their first growing season.*
Clear out any deficiencies that you are certain will
    impede growth.
Assume that what's left is sound and well intentioned.
Things want to move towards wholeness;
but they need to find out, first, who they are.

So do people.

PURIM

Explanation of words, phrases, and concepts
appearing in the
Purim poems

PURIM, or the Feast of Lots, is a joyous holiday that usually falls in late-February or mid-March, which celebrates the saving of the Jews from a threatened massacre during the Persian period (539-330 BCE.) The *Purim* story is told in the **Book of Esther**, whose eponymous heroine plays the leading role in saving her people. Interestingly, The Book of Esther never mentions God.

Purim is traditionally celebrated with exuberance and includes gift-giving to friends and poor people. Jews — including rabbis — wear costumes to look like characters from the *Purim* story when the story is read aloud in synagogue, and they are encouraged to drink liquor until they can't distinguish between two of the major Purim characters, **Haman**, the villain, and **Mordecai**, a palace official, and Esther's cousin, who is one of the heroes of Purim. Also, the congregation is supposed to drown out Haman's name whenever it is mentioned by making a lot of noise, either using noisemakers called *gragers*, or by stamping their feet, hissing, or booing.

For *bimah,* see Hanukkah explanations.

In many synagogues, *Purim* is celebrated as a holiday primarily aimed at **children**. But some adults — including parents — would like a meaningful adult celebration, either instead of, or in addition to, one for children.

Eunuchs appear in every chapter of the Book of Esther, and take on many different roles. Hathach is a eunuch who carries messages between Esther and Mordecai, helping them figure out what to do about Haman's genocide plot.

The day before Purim is a minor **fast** day in the Jewish calendar. No one, including Queen Esther, was allowed to speak to King Ahasuerus unless he had summoned that person to him. So to purify herself and get in touch with her own courage to confront the king, Esther and all the Jews in Shushan fast for three days.

***Hamantashen** — literally, "Haman's hats" — are triangular-shaped cookies filled with fruit or jam that are eaten on *Purim*. Common fillings include *lekvar* (prune), *mun*, (poppy seed), cherry, and apricot.

Havdalah is the ceremony that ends *Shabbat* on Saturday night.

Long ago wealthy or aristocratic people would recline or **lean** while they ate.

****Lekvar* is pureed, cooked prune filling used in hamantashen. *Mun* is a sweetened poppy seed mixture used to fill hamantashen.

***A *megillah* is a long or complicated story; anything that is done in its fullest form, from start to finish. Capitalized, the *Megillah* refers to The Book of Esther.

***A *minyan* is a gathering of ten people, the minimum necessary for a communal religious service according to Jewish law.

Pesach is the Hebrew word for Passover.

A **sestina** is complex French verse form, with six stanzas of six lines and a final triplet, all stanzas having the same six words at the line-ends in six different sequences that follow a fixed pattern, and with all six words appearing in the closing three-line envoi.

*****Shalach manot** are goodie bags containing *hamantashen*, candy, fruit, and other treats that are given to family, friends, and needy people on *Purim*.

*****Shuckle** means to sway back and forth during prayer or *Torah* study.

A *shul* is a synagogue.

It was in the palace of **Shushan** that Queen Esther outmaneuvered Haman and saved the Jews of the Persian Empire.

*****Tzedakah**, which literally means "righteousness," often refers to charity, but the concept actually embraces a bigger principle of doing good to ensure that the needs of others are met.

Although Esther is usually seen as the heroine of *Purim*, Queen **Vashti**, too, is important. She refused the orders of her husband, King Ahasuerus, to display herself at a drunken feast in front of the king and his dignitaries and noblemen. As a result of her stance, King Ahasuerus demotes her and soon holds a beauty contest to find a replacement for Vashti. The winner? Esther. Vashti is now thought of as an early feminist.

Esther was a **vegetarian**.

***Definition from the *Dictionary of Jewish Words*.
See **page xxv** for more information.

Purim: In the Pre-Spring

Just this week
the snowdrops departed
after having told us
the groundhog was right
and what oppresses us, passes.

Just this week
the crocuses, little cups of yellow, purple, and
    white, appeared,
their determination, even when there's still snow on
    the ground, reminding us
that color hibernates,
but always reawakens.

Just this week
the daffodil stems extended themselves
demonstrating patience, and possibility,
and the expectation of a day
when all of a sudden, flowers will bloom.

The Book of Esther

It's the only book of the Bible
with no mention of God's name.
That's because we see it
on faces delighted to be in *shul*;
and we smell it
in the sweetness of early spring;
and we taste it
in the buttery yellow dough of *hamantashen,*
and the intensity of *lekvar,* or *mun;*
and we feel it
in that moment we discover a *shalach manot* at
   our doorstep;
and we hear it
in the stomps and shouts and whistles and *gragers*
and in between, every word of the story.

All our senses are engaged
which is another way
of being with God
even without a name.

Been There, Done That

I've heard the words of the *Megillah*
over and over
and over the noise of shouter-outers
every year
so it would be easy to say
that I don't have to go back
because I know the story
and its morals
and its lessons
and its customs.

But that's like saying
I know what it's like to see a robin build its nest
from the castaways of grey winter,
or to see spring's first family of goslings
bobbing in the slime of the neighborhood pond,
so it doesn't matter if I doze off
and miss the earth's reawakening.

But that's like saying
I've been in love
and know the progression of falling in it
and then out
so it doesn't matter if I deep freeze my battered heart
and miss what might be for keeps.

 But that's like saying
I've gone through the year-round cycle of the *Torah*
over and over
and I've heard the important stories
repeatedly
        — and a lot of it is filler, anyway,
        like who begat whom
        and the dimensions and materials of building
                holy places —

so it doesn't matter if I tune out
and miss what might have meaning.

If I close the door on *Purim*
because I've been there and done that
I miss the little crumbs of awareness
that can enrich my holiday
like an extra scoop of sugar in the *mun* filling:

> like the tradition of eating chickpeas
> because that's what Esther ate
> to keep Kosher in the palace;

and the rounding-out notion that Haman had a
  wife, Zeresh,
who was maybe as beautiful as Esther
and defiant, finally, as Vashti,
and that maybe he knew love
and even gave it;

> and that *Purim* must continue
> even after the Messiah comes
> to remind us
> that even though something is over
> and we're on to the next
> we have to keep re-experiencing
> and re-enacting
> to remain open

to the little bits and particles that may be new to us
but have been there all the time
that can make all the difference
even in this moving-fast-and-forward world.

Tipsy Rabbis

It's good to see
tipsy rabbis
who let down their hair
or hide it under a Marilyn wig
or a crayoned construction-paper crown,
their chins hidden by Mordecai's cottony beard
that absorbs their vodka breath like a surgical sponge,
while they prance and trot and vogue
      although not quite Jagger
by the *bimah,*
in the same setting
where solemnity rules, like Ahasuerus,
      but without all the layers of advisors in between
      (unless you count the synagogue board
      who may or may not be in attendance.)

It's good for tipsy rabbis
to be seen, close up,
      in sniffing distance,
by their congregants,
as they lose their voices over the racket of erasing
  a name
made by Halloween-y children
in Hollywood costumes and superhero get-ups
and their parents, who've handed over their
    playfulness like *tzedakah* to their kids,
as the rabbis unzip their everyday sobriety,
and temporarily shed some shoulds about being
    appropriately rabbinic

and figuratively speaking, step off the *bimah*,
and unlike this service, in which someone's name
   is effaced,
      they're allowed to claim their own names,
      to act their secular selves,
      to show their flip side
      like a reversible jacket,
      where the lining can be brighter than the shell.

Sound

We've been ordered
to hear the Book of Esther.
We've been commanded
to open up our ears
to let in the story, and its truth.

It's as important as the other rule:
to open up our mouths
to drown out the name, and its sound.

But when do we know we've been loud enough
    to erase?
And when do we know we've listened well enough
    to hear?

Rules

It is written:
Reading the *Megillah* in any but the original language
   is to be avoided.
It is written:
The *Megillah* must be read standing and from the
   scroll, not the heart.
     Which is why this must be written:

Heaven forbid I should translate
or make up-to-date
or paraphrase
or annotate.
God forbid I should sit
or lean like *Pesach*
or slouch
or squat.
God forbid I should memorize
or interpret
or feel
or read between the lines.
     The story is strong enough to withstand,
     The story is strong enough to stand with,

and if it's not,
why care about the rules
if we are reading something
that doesn't speak to us?

Sour Gripes Make Good Wine

I apologize,
upfront,
to the parents of children
who dress up in gauze and crowns
and forbidden lipstick
and premature beards
like Halloween.

Their little Esthers and Hamans make noise above
and beyond what's necessary to drown out the
   wicked name,
      which is right,
but not for so long and loud
that I can't hear the words of the reader,
      which is my right.

I apologize to the parents
who fear, who feel,
      children must have fun in synagogue,
      or they'll leave the fold,
that everything must be sweet
like Mary Poppins's spoonful of sugar,
like the *hamantashen*, gone
by the time I reach the table with the baked goods.

Their adorable Mordecais and Vashtis go home
having learned

that their parents have given them the holiday
like a *shalach manot* gift
    because their parents have bought into the notion
    that once you have children
    you give up your own connection,
to Purim.

And you'll say to me,
    Wait until you have children,
    you'll see,

And I say,
    Wait, you'll see
    how I take this *hamantashen* dough
    and shape it into the requisite tricorns,
    hats of many sizes,
    one of which could fit my adult head,
    too.

Hamantashen, or I'll Eat My Hat

George Washington and Haman
had something in common:
Both wore three-cornered hats.

Washington, the patriotic patriarch
    who, it seems, slept around America,
    had a superego that couldn't tolerate lies,
    and an early eco-awareness, perhaps,
    about the consequences of hacking down trees —
wore a tricorn.

Haman, the sinister prime minister
who had it in for the Jews
    as well as an extermination plan
    like rat poison,
    easily accessible, under the kitchen sink
wore one, too.

Both the pole that Haman was impaled on
and the ax that felled the cherry tree
are sharp enough
to cut pie crust.

Eat cherry pie as you remember
and let each piece fuel you to action.

But eat *hamantashen* with the gusto of a sadist,
like a rabid raccoon let loose in a barnyard,
to obliterate not just Haman's name
    but the hat that sat on his head,
    housing his hatred.

Even Women

Even women are commanded
to hear the *Megillah*
    which is odd
      for a people who, in the name of easing
        the burdens
    of motherhood and homemaking,
    regularly let women off the hook
      of participation,
    thus keeping them from giving to
      the community,
    let alone getting.
Maybe it's because women know how to focus
    turning into all eyes, and all ears
    to tune into their children in the middle of
  tumult and din,
    like at a *Megillah* reading.
Or maybe it's because of the starring roles of women
  in the story:
    The brave Vashti,
    who we've adopted even though she's other,
    and cunning Esther,
    the only queen any of us ever imagined we
      could become.

The Eunuch Carries the Message Back and Forth

I
It's quiet in Shushan.
Sshh.

II
I have no voice, mouths Esther
I have no power
I may not speak unless spoken to
like a child
is how my husband treats me
like a child
I must be summoned
like every child, woman and man
he could kill me
if I talked
if I told him who I am.

III
Don't hesitate
Make noise
Be loud
Find sound

IV
I eat no food, says Esther
I drink no water
I will not take nourishment until I choose
like a woman
I understand food
like a woman

I decide for myself
like every child, man, and woman

I might kill him
if I ate,
if I chewed and spit gristle and bones.
    So I'll lock my mouth for three days
    and my body will release what doesn't make
        me strong.

Vashti

said no
refused the summons
would not appear
like a beck-and-call Barbie
by her husband
and his cronies
all of whom stunk of moldy clothes and old wine
and were eager to own her with their eyes
as a mannequin for jewels
and conquered flesh.
and when she said no
refused the summons
would not appear
her husband swelled with rage
(and his sidekick warned that if the beans spilled,
    other women would feel free to decline)
so he cut her away like an apple bruise
and threw her out like what was left from dinner
to the dogs and rats and other scroungers
and once he dried out
and realized he was longing
he went to Atlantic City
and picked a winner in a tiara
sent her to a spa
then took her home
never knowing her name
not knowing that her name
if translated from a language he'd never understand
means no,
never,
again, no.

Sestina for Women at Purim

1

It's the only holiday when there's no mention of
  God's name
and when women, not just men, are commanded
  to listen
to every word of the entire *Megillah*.
In return, like men, they're allowed to make noise and
  get drunk
and dress up in costume, maybe as Queen Esther,
and eat what they no doubt baked: the *hamantashen*.

2

There's nothing like a straight-from-the-
  oven *hamantashen*.
It's comforting and sweet, like whispering
  God's name.
Poor Queen Esther;
in her court she had to listen
(without the benefit of getting drunk)
to lots of men telling braggart stories — not
  in whispers — each with his very own
  endless *megillah*.

3

It would take a book the size of the *Megillah*
to write down all the different recipes for
  hamantashen.
It can be fun to bake when you're drunk,
but you have to be careful not to say something bad
  in God's name.
I wonder what it would be like to listen
to the women's stories shared in the kitchen of
  Queen Esther.

4

She liked to write, Queen Esther,
and wrote her memoir, her own *megillah*.
She forced the men in her court to listen,
— while they sipped wine and nibbled
    hamantashen —
as she read her story, which left out God's name.
Oy: It sounded like when she wrote it she must have
    been drunk.

5

It's not like you have to get drunk
to write something bad, even if you're as apparently
    untalented as Queen Esther.
But before you start to write, if you whisper
    God's name,
you, too, might be able to write your own *megillah*.
Don't postpone writing by baking *hamantashen* —
and make sure your family listens.

6

At *Purim*, it might be fascinating to listen
to the ramblings of a Jewish woman who's drunk.
She might recite from memory her recipe
    for *hamantashen*
or even if she's costumed as Queen Esther
she might finally tell her own story, her own *megillah*.
It may or may not mention God's name.

7
So in God's name, I urge you to listen
to women who write their own *megillahs* — and you
    don't need to get drunk —
to toast women telling their stories, including Queen
    Esther's — and ladies, write more, and spend less
    time baking *hamantashen*!

Even If

Even if life has left you alone
and you're isolated, say, in a tiny town in Alaska,
or a room in an old-age home,
or a family where no one eats together
        or even in the folds of your mind,
you're still supposed to read the *Megillah*,
the whole thing,
every word,
even if you can't get to a *minyan*
        or you're blind,
        and have to read it by hearing the words,
you're still supposed to interpret
Purim's tale of cleverness layered on oppression
like Jif slathered on a slice of Wonder,

which is odd
for a Diaspora people who insist on community
and discourage words of worship at home
        even to the point of confessing en masse
        our most intimate misdeeds, last year's resolute
                words gone rancid.

So the only way this works — for me —
is that *Purim* exists because Vashti said no
and Esther spoke when she wasn't supposed to.
        Two women who each took a stand, aloud;
        two women who each took a stand, alone.

Shalach Manot

The first time you surprised me with a package
I couldn't imagine what I'd done
or what special day it was
to inspire the gift.

It contained:
 A teeny box of Sun-Maid raisins
 Three small *hamantashen* you'd bought
  in Brookline
 A Baggie of mint lentils (the candy you
  hoarded, teasing, in a glass jar)
 and a few pennies,
and was left, unsigned,
in a brown paper bag
as if by Santa
or more likely, given the season,
the Easter bunny.

When you explained it to me
I kept seeing parallels between Purim and Halloween
 like dressing up, out of character and
  into another,
 and sweets,
 and the flip-flop tension between evil and good.
And then I tried to figure out why you'd given the gift
 to me
since you only have to present *shalach manot* of at
 least two foods to one
  person

and I was never sure if I was your favorite;
was it because you knew my other name is Esther
or because you knew what knowledge hadn't been
    passed along to me?

So many things I learned from you:
Like wearing white for *Yom Kippur*, and no leather,
and how to douse the *Havdalah* candles in wine,
and that people bought Kosher toothpaste for *Pesach*.
Like how to *shuckle* with prayer, moving to the rhythm
    of the words,
and how to invite, then welcome, the white noise of
    Sabbath,
and dress up Saturday lunch, and elongate it, then
    nap.

So I want to thank you for the present
and what you taught me in the past
about how to be a Jew
like maybe my grandparents — or before — knew,
and even though I pared back to being me
(then added other layers, slowly, and organically)
I hope someone has given you gifts
that surprise and enrich you
and make you eager to open brown paper bags
which, you've learned to imagine,
may well contain something sweet.

Tzedakah

When I give *tzedakah*
I feel rich.
Somehow, the act of giving
     even something small, like *shalach manot,*
gives me a feeling of wealth
and generosity
of wallet and of spirit.

But *tzedakah* is about more than giving money;
it's about trusting that the universe regenerates
and that a lopped-off limb
grows back.
I couldn't have given *tzedakah* years ago,
not in the real sense,
and it's not that I was ever teetering on poverty.
But after years of believing
that an empty bowl would remain empty
and a well might well run dry
I finally feel
that I am more than enough
to give
without risking my own disappearance.

And on the Other 364 Days

It's all fine
and well
to stand up against oppression
when you're wearing a costume
and alcohol has made you more yourself
        or maybe less so
but for the other 364 days
you are commanded
        by The Book of What's Right,
        which all religions subscribe to
to stand up against oppression
in your everyday clothes
and your sobriety
when you're clear-headed
        and -hearted
and can recognize the difference
between who should be blessed
and who should be cursed,

and to skim off *Purim's* skin of hysteria
        like fat globules in a pot of soup
and see the persecution that simmers,
    still, underneath.

The Next Steps

It's not enough to bury Haman in noise.
We have to outshout the names of all oppressors
    and drown out their sounds.

It's not enough to bury the names of oppressors.
We have to oust them from power
    and drown them in the sea.

It's not enough to bury the damage they did.
We have to air it out, and shake it out
    so we don't drown the memories and
        forget them.

And then, buoyant,
quiet, but breathing deeply,
we have to take the next steps:
Repair,
and prevent.

PASSOVER

Explanation of words, phrases, and concepts appearing in the Passover poems

PASSOVER is an eight-day-long holiday in spring that celebrates the exodus of the Jews from slavery in Egypt, and their passage to the Promised Land of Israel.

Afikoman is a piece of *matzah* hidden early in the Passover *seder*. When the meal is over, the children search for the *afikoman* and the one who finds it wins a small prize, either money or a toy. In some families, the *afikoman* is hidden in a special fabric sleeve used only for this purpose.

A *blech* is a metal sheet placed over the burners on a stove to retain heat to keep food and water warm during *Shabbat*. My mother, however, used it to make our stovetop "Kosher enough" for Passover for her father's approval.

Chicken soup with matzah balls is a standard feature of many *seder* meals.

Children's table — At large seders, the children often sit together at their own table.

Dayenu — literally "it would have been enough." A traditional *seder* song, *Dayenu* deals with how much God could have done to save the Jews before it would have been enough, each miracle followed by the chorus of *"Dayenu."*

At the *seder*, the door is opened for **Elijah the Prophet**, who will bring peace to the world.

Elisha is Elijah's successor.

At a *seder*, it is traditional for the youngest attendee to ask the **Four Questions**, which explain Passover's symbols and meaning.

Also at the *seder,* there is a section in which, traditionally, **four sons** ask questions about observing the holiday: A wise son, a wicked son, a simple son, and one who did not know how to ask.

Gefilte fish, which is basically an oval fish patty, doesn't look much like fish by the time it reaches the *seder* table; pike, carp, and whitefish are commonly used. Lots of *bubbes* tell stories — *bubbe meises* (For bubbe and bubbe meises, see Hanukkah explanations) of buying the live fish and letting it swim in the bathtub until cooking time.

***A *haggadah* is the small book of liturgy, prayers, songs, and rituals used at a Passover *seder; haggadot* is plural.

Hametz refers to the food that's not permitted to be eaten during Passover. People clean their houses, and put away *hametz*, to various degrees. There is a formal search for *hametz* that takes place right after sundown on the night before Passover. A blessing is said, and the search is done by candlelight or flashlight, with a small bag to sweep up the crumbs, usually by using a feather. It is customary to place crumbs in a few places where they can be easily found. They are burned the following morning.

Hametz can also be thought of as generic excess because of the time it needs to rise before baking.

***Haroset** is a mixture of apples, sweet red wine, and chopped nuts that is placed on the *seder* plate at Passover. It is symbolic of the mortar and bricks the ancient Israelites used to build the pyramids when they were slaves in Egypt.

Although there are more sophisticated **Jewish wines** available, it just seems right to drink the traditional wines at *seders*. I grew up with the sweetest of the sweet, Manischewitz's Concord Grape, sometimes lovingly referred to as "cough medicine."

K'nock, the way my mother used it, means to hit. It might have been related to *k'nocker*, a Yiddish word for someone who thinks of himself — or herself — with an unusually big ego.

Leaning at the *seder* is explained that since we were slaves in Egypt and now we are free, we must act according to our new status.

The **Leviathan** can be thought of as a huge sea monster that will be killed when the Messiah comes. In some versions of the story, after it is killed its flesh will be served as a feast for righteous people, and its skin used to cover the tent where the banquet will take place.

When *Pharaoh* finally allows the Jews to leave Egypt, they leave in such a hurry that they don't have time for their bread to rise; thus, they eat unleavened bread, ***matzah***.

In recent years, **Miriam**'s role in the Passover story has finally been recognized: Moses led the people; Aaron gave the speeches for Moses, who either had a stutter or was just not an eloquent speaker; but it was Miriam, some believe, who actually put the words together.

Moshe is the Hebrew word for Moses.

Nahshon was the first person who, on faith, stepped into the Red Sea, trusting that the waters would part.

The **Red Sea**, or Sea of Reeds, is the body of water the Israelites crossed following their exodus from Egypt. The appropriate translation of the Hebrew phrase *Yam Suph* is disputed, as is the exact location referred to.

***A *seder* is the traditional, ceremonial dinner on Passover.

*****Shehecheyanu** is the blessing that thanks God for long life and for reaching a happy occasion.

Shifra and Puah were two Jewish midwives.

Shmaltz is rendered chicken fat, used as shortening (before people knew to worry about clogging up their arteries.)

A **shtickel** is a Yiddish word meaning "small amount."

For *ta'am,* see Hanukkah explanations.

There's a section of the Passover *seder* when participants dip a finger in a glass of wine and spill **ten drops** to acknowledge the plagues that befell the Egyptians.

***Definition from the *Dictionary of Jewish Words.*
See **page xxv** for more information.

PASSOVER

Early-Spring Flowers

This is the time of year
when I'm especially glad I have a nose:
Mostly — after the empty smell of winter —
for the early-spring flowers,
like hyacinths, lilacs, and lilies of the valley,
whose fragrances are thick,
almost shocking,
and as intoxicating as Passover wine.

When we open the door for Elijah
the fragrance of those early-spring flowers
sneaks inside, like party crashers on tiptoe.
They mix with my mother's tea-rose perfume
and the smell of baked chicken,
and wrap themselves around us like a big man's *tallit*
to remind us that we've seen the back of winter
and the world is outside, beginning to bloom.

Waiting For Pesach/Sid's Dayenu

There wasn't much time for the dough to rise.
His body was eating itself up
sucking its own marrow
gripping naked nerves with its teeth
wrinkling in
turning the color of wet cement.
But he threw his arms around a stop sign
and held against the onslaught of waters

until that first night
when he sat, cushioned, at the head of the table
bald, a walnut shell,
a king among them,
and sang through the grey
a story he told each year
and finally, at the other side,
finally, it was enough.

My friend, Sid Altman, died of cancer on April 14, 1996, just a
few days after leading his family's Passover *seder.*

Crumbs I

My mother shlepped the *hametz* downstairs
to the basement,
lined the kitchen shelves with paper,
replaced utensils,
scrubbed,
and covered surfaces with tin foil
and a *blech,* used incorrectly, on the stovetop,
all for her father's inspection.

But there were always crumbs,
like white-glove dust,
that refused to let go,
that hung on like a judgment,
because, her father would scold,
— dry spittle at the corners of his mouth —
she didn't use a feather
to search out and discard crumbs,
that she wasn't doing enough
or the right way,
to find those stubborn crumbs,
which refused to be rounded up;
like a cattle-drive renegade,
they remained
for anyone who knew where to look, to see,
he would say.

I don't do all that
to get ready for Passover,
and I don't worry about crumbs, no matter who
— even the spirit of my grandfather, if that's possible —
might be looking.

Hametz

Hametz is all the things we can live without:
the puff, the fluff,
the excess stuff,
the icing on the cake and, in most cases,
the cake itself,
the overboard, the elaborate,
the non-essential,
the too-too, the frou-frou,
the Bloomingdale's when Sears would do,
the Range Rover when a Subaru would get you
    there, too,
the centerpiece which, in fact,
prevents you from seeing across the table,
the lazy that takes its time rising
because it knows no one's going anywhere

so even as we congratulate ourselves for getting
    along without *hametz*
for eight days,
like a Yom Kippur fast,
let's thank Someone for our luck
that we have the *hametz* to do without,
that we can choose
to pare down for a week,
trusting, knowing with certainty,
that *hametz* will be there to return to
that we don't have to do without
that we have yeast and sugar,
that we have water and time.

Soup

My *bubbe*
who passed away two months after
    President Kennedy was killed
keeps company with me in the kitchen
every year
when I make matzoh balls.
Wearing an apron around her waist — I don't —
her thin, white hair in a loose, low bun
her feet achy, in scuffs,
her skin like my mother's face,
her nose with the dent like all the Frankel girls,
her fingertips red,

She urges me to use salt
and *shmaltz*, better for taste — I don't —
and to mold little balls
because they puff up like pride
in the stock, hers chicken, mine mock,
after they rise and float
and to slice the carrots diagonal
and the celery straight
for contrast
and to give the men two,
the biggest,
and the children one,
and to skim off the fat but not all, for *ta'am*
and to serve it "piping hot"
as if to President Kennedy, he should rest in peace.

Soup-making skipped a generation
in my family
so she smiles her tired smile

the one I know from photos,
adjusts her steel spectacles upwards,
urges me, again, to wear an apron — I don't —
and as the soup simmers,
escaping as mist,
she disappears as it rises and floats.

Crumbs II

It was all orchestrated by the mother.
Moments before dark on the night before the
   first *seder*
she scattered breadcrumbs around her
   linoleum kitchen
but not leading anywhere, like Hansel and Gretl's
   way home.

It was black inside like a fairytale woods, so
each person lit a candle, searching in its orange glow
for those deliberate crumbs
of day-old doughnuts or the last *shtickel* of challah
from Friday night.

Illuminated, you'd search the kitchen's corners,
deep in the nooks and the slits of the crannies,
searching for the crumbs your mother planted.
You'd have a feather, or an old toothbrush –
its bristles splayed like a newborn giraffe's legs —
and when you found something, you'd brush it
onto yesterday's news, or into a little paper bag.

The next morning, you'd burn it,
letting the crumbs devour themselves to nothing —
like the marshmallow that falls off your stick
and into the fire,
     leaving behind only a smell that reminds you
      of something that used to be there, but is
        no more.

Grandpa's Seders I

I didn't understand Grandpa's *seders*
He was deaf
and mumbled
and shuffled
and had dried phlegm at the corners of his mouth.
We used *haggadot* from the kosher wine companies
    they weren't all the same
written all in Hebrew
all sizes
with a photo of the Dome of the Rock on the cover,
stained with years of wine and chicken broth.

I sat on one of the hard high-backed chairs
covered in mustard-colored oilcloth
in the dark dining room with the fake fireplace
that glowed like night eyes with the flick of a switch.
No one tried to draw me out
or in
and my brother always asked the questions
even though I was younger,
and there weren't any prizes
or reckoning.

After I became a bat mitzvah at 29,
I asked my father, who was thrilled
    and, I believe, relieved
that I wanted to lead the *seder*.
Soon, once I owned my own home,
I housed the *seder*, too, cooking,
then cleaning the dishes and the linens,
(embroidered by my *bubbe*, the tablecloth was
stained, year upon year, by drips of Manischewitz.)

Being single, I was making the holiday,
and I was making it my own.
Not everyone did that;
some still don't.

I had a choice back then:
I could have kept my feet in Brooklyn
like an old soul in lace-up orthopedic shoes.

But I chose to take off honking,
   like a pack of spring geese;
I chose imagination,
I choose imagination, still.

Crumbs III

I like this ritual,
this Jewish spring cleaning,
getting rid of the crumbs in my life,
the pieces that don't add up to much
and have gone stale.

Once upon a time, I loved someone
who wouldn't let me eat a doughnut in his car
and, several decades later,
offered me crumbs of friendship.
At first I accepted them gratefully
— hungrily — but after a time
I realized that even an endless supply of crumbs
didn't add up, and
didn't satisfy me as much as one intact cookie,
    even a boring little ginger snap,
    or some other intrinsically unattractive sweet.

So I'm telling you
when I open the door for Elijah this year
I'm not going to let just any one in,
even if it's Elijah's guest, if he comes empty-handed.

And even when Passover has passed,
if I'm going to let you in,
you have to bring me some of those buttery bakery
  cookies
that look like pastel-painted leaves,
or better yet, an entire cake,
one you know I like.
You see, I don't accept crumbs any more.

Grandpa's Seders II

My grandfather's *seders*
didn't speak to me
My grandfather
didn't speak to me
My grandfather
only spoke Yiddish
My grandfather
couldn't hear
My grandfather
came here from Europe
My grandfather
never heard my voice

And what I wanted to say,
what I wanted him to hear,
was that I wanted his *seders* to speak
to
me.

Haiku for Carp

Swimming in the tub
not knowing what it will be:
the *gefilte* fish.

What is *"gefilte"*?
Not showing where it comes from?
Where are its gills, mouth?

Mama *k'nocks* its head
(This is a woman who hates
to look at road kill.)

Some love the jelly
like a bodily fluid.
Others shy away.

Packed in a glass jar
the creature it was before
is invisible.

Packed in a glass jar
Passover, itself, sometimes,
needs to be set free.

Jewish Wine

Jewish wine is sweet wine:
Thick like cough medicine,
unsophisticated as a greenhorn,
and sweet, life should be sweet,
not dry like France or California,
intensely fruity, as if thousands of grapes devoured
   each other,
with a no-frills screw-off cap,
and it's ghettoed to the far corners of liquor shops.

It is not the kind you store in a wine rack
upside down, on a tilt,
to keep the cork wet,
not the type you go to adult-ed classes to learn about
or vineyards to taste
or read about in magazines,
not something you save for special occasions,
or to pass on like jewelry or old-country linens,
or to leave a fancy job for, to make your own,
like a gentleman wealthy enough to hire
   vineyard workers.

But it warms on the way down
like an old friend's embrace,
and settles in your feet, insisting that you dance
even if you're sitting.
It settles in your fingers, which feel drowsy like a
   Shabbat nap,
and in your head,
where the walls come down,

and even your rough-edged cousin softens when
   she's lit,
like candles,
like a honey-bright holiday.

The Children's Table

The children's table
always had plates from another set
and the odd forks and spoons
and shaky legs
and the tablecloth that barely spilled over the edges
    and the spilled-wine stains
and the soup filled only half-way up
and the white-meat chicken slices
and the grape juice 'til you sneaked wine
and the lumpy leftover puddles of gefilte jelly
and the kids' *haggadot* with drawings of *Moshe*, staff
  in hand,
and the delight-in-disgust enthusiasm for the plagues
and the dread of who's-the-youngest for the
  four questions
and the fight to find the *afikoman*, to barter
and the parted waters separating it from the
  grown ups
    with their matched sets
    and silver
    and almost-thick-as-honey Concord grape
  and the choice of dark or light

Reach out across the divide
to the children at that separate little table
and make something about Passover
— a song, a story, a bowl of soup —
memorable.
At that table sits the future of the Jewish people.

Four Questions

Why must the man still lead the *seder*
    when, like Moses, he's not a good reader
    and doesn't much care
    and eats bagels by the fourth day, anyway

Why must the woman still make the preparations
    when, like a slave, she works full time
    and *shleps* the kids and coordinates schedules
    and doesn't like to cook, anyway

Why must the youngest still ask the questions
    when, like Aaron, she's just a mouthpiece
    and performs only for praise
    and is too young to understand, anyway

Why must all who gather expect the same *seder* from
  year to year
    when, like Shifra and Puah, they know how
       to midwife
    and could bring the story to life
    and set it, finally, free.

Shifra and Pu'ah Saved the Boys

The midwives lied
    an aberration like murder
    from women who always tell the painful truth.
They fast-forwarded the birth speed,
compressing the gut-splitting body rip of delivery,
reporting that Jewish women's juices flowed faster
  than a flood
and declaring their own incompetence to keep up.

But what about the Jewish baby girls who weren't
  marked for death?
They grew up without brothers,
with mothers with holes in their hearts,
    grieving, unspoken, for someone always missing,
with fathers who remained inside themselves
    with no one to teach boy-things to.

So here's one time when being a Jewish girl
was better than being a Jewish boy.
Hooray! Finally!
But not really.
Girls, growing in that love-stunted world,
    with parents whose hacked-off arms
        couldn't hug,
    whose mutilated tongues couldn't speak,
    never fully came alive
    and died little deaths throughout their lives.

Miriam the Speechwriter

Moses, awkward of voice, chose to be mute,
Aaron delivered,
but it was Miriam who put the words in his mouth,
words that flowed like honey of bees that sting,
sweet enough to make the message palatable,
thick enough to spread through the crowd,
and golden, reflecting
     and reminding of the calf.
Miriam the speechwriter is remembered most
  for dancing
but she was the one who gave voice,
who swallowed the clouds and spit them out
  in letters,
who translated God to People,
and moved them to reconsider and repent.

A woman's words, ghostly and potent.
A woman's voice, heard only if spoken by a man.

Enough/Dip Ten Times

There's always enough of the bad things:
>Pain
>War
>Sorrow
>A child's death
>Humiliation
>Terror
>Animal abuse
>Loss
>Prejudice
>and Injustice

And often enough of some things which, in limited
amounts, bring happiness:
>Possessions
>Chocolate
>House guests
>Exercise
>TV
>Trying new things
>Travel
>Sex
>Daydreaming
>Sitting in the sun

But is there ever enough of the truly good things?
>Joy
>Flexibility
>Dancing uninhibitedly
>Love
>Discovery
>Tenderness

The ability to make someone laugh
Compassion
Friendship
and Tolerance

Enough is a relative matter,
a continuum,
between wanting it all and being satisfied
  with smaller.
If you want less, enough comes sooner,
and if you'll never be content, enough
  grows enormous.

The trick, as with all things that matter, is the balance,
to fight the right battles,
to give up, and in, on the lesser,
and fold like poker,
and to hold out, when sufficient is not enough.

Nahshon

Someone has to be the first one
to test the waters:
Even if you can't swim, and can't imagine floating,
to dip a big toe in the ocean;
Even if the opposite shore is invisible, far
  beyond imagination,
to extend yourself;
Even if the sea is icy, with floes, and muck,
to take the first step;
Even without a life preserver, or inflatable raft, or
  water wings,
to risk total immersion;
Even if everyone else says no, and holds back in terror;
to plunge in,
trusting you'll survive the depths.

What if Nahshon Didn't Know How to Swim

When I finish my laps at the pool
I lean back, let go, and float
and imagine that God's big hand is below me
holding me, cupping me like a cool drink from
   a stream.

Nahshon didn't know what might take place
— he was beyond knowing, and below it —
when he took that first step into the Sea of Reeds.
Nothing happened
except his hot, tired feet felt the relief of water.
Nahshon took another step,
up to his dusty ankles,
and nothing happened.
Then to his knees,
and thighs,
and belly,
step by step,
further, beyond,
step by step by step, deeper, darker, down.
Then, holding his breath, he became buoyant
and it was only when the water was up to his nostrils
that the Sea of Reeds separated like a newborn from
   her mother.

In case they might have to split seas again,
Nahshon, father of many sons,
made sure he taught them how to swim.

To Take the First Step

Before we'd take the first step
all of us would need a lifejacket
and aqua-socks against the jaggedy ocean floor
and an inflatable tube
and waterproof sunblock, SPF infinity,
and wrap-around shades from L.L. Bean
and a hat that deflects sun
and a Swiss army knife with the toolbox of
    attachments
and Red Cross-certified confidence
and a pack of space-age dehydrated food
and a camel's hump of spring water
and a send-off of marathon-watching cheers
and a week's notice so we could cancel the paper
and eat up the perishables
and arrange for the dog

>   but by that time, the door would have dissolved
>   the cleft receded
>   the mirage evaporated

and the trio you can't touch:
        conviction
        fearlessness
        and faith
would have melted in the desert sun
and been sucked up by the sand.

To Find the Afikoman

To find the *afikoman*
you have to play what it would feel like
to be the matzoh
— fragile into fragments, bumpy, almost only
   two dimensional —
and where you would feel safe,
blanketed someplace between,
somewhere soft and cushiony,
inserted and slipped in like a DVD

you have to imagine what it would feel like
to be the household head who hides it
— who doesn't want the house wrecked, the secrets
   in drawers discovered —
and where you would feel you'd been fair in hiding it,
balancing too easy and impossible,
hoping for few crumbs

you have to envision what it would feel like
to be the prize money
— cool, textured coins, bills still damp with sweat —
and where you would feel honored as the prize,
knowing you leave home to go with the winner,
who you'll stay with a short time
before you're given away, again,
and have to leave home.

When The Messiah Comes,
The Leviathan Will Die

There'll be enough scraps of salty skin
for a handbag big enough
to hold everything.

    No longer
    will the sea be fearful,
its large mouth having been
erased from between spineless reeds,
its triangular bifurcated tail having been
stilled, to the relief of ambergrisy sailors,
its scaly bulk having been
split open, mercilessly, unzipped.
      The greyness has risen, like the wizard;
      the skin smoothes out under the sun.

She comes along with her knife, a switch
blade, cutting away the excess like piecrust.
Denied leather shop in junior high, she is surprised at
  how easily
skin is pierced, how it falls apart
and away
from itself.
What's left is a large rectangle
which, on orders, she drapes over the roof.
It falls unevenly, like a quilt on the bed,
a little too much to one side
but sufficient.

With the extra
she goes to her grandmother's Singer
and sews together the pieces of a shawl
which she wears
when she dives into the sea
to search for dessert:
Leviathan's intact heart.

Waiting for Elijah: Plan B

I'm sick of waiting for Elijah.
I'm tired of opening the door every year
    and the only thing that rushes in is early-spring
        night air.
I've had enough of hoping to be rescued
    and looking for a sign that times are on the brink.
I've had my fill of imagining a man
    ushering in the new era,
    and nibbling at the carrot I never get to finish.
I'm bored with singing his song because he's not
  coming to claim it,
and I don't like how we've given over, and wait from
  year to year.

Go, get Elisha, and escort him to our table.

Let him join us as we drink Elijah's wine,

then turn our hearts inside out
    and storm the arid land, and grab chunks of
        crumbly freedom.

Let's ride in on wheels of fire,
and wrestle from a mirage
water for the parched,
huts for the homeless,
and then maybe,
maybe,
Elijah will join us.

COUNTING OF THE OMER

Explanation of words, phrases, and concepts appearing in the
Lag b'Omer/ Counting of the Omer poems

LAG B'OMER is a minor holiday celebrated on the 33rd day after Passover. For observant Jews, it is the one day between Passover and *Shavuot* when little boys who turn three years old are allowed to get a haircut. The most well-known custom of *Lag b'Omer* is lighting bonfires throughout Israel, often explained as a way to honor Rabbi Shimon bar Yochai, whose teachings brought spiritual light to the world.

For **Azazel,** see *Yom Kippur* explanations.

***A *mohel* is the person trained to perform ritual circumcision, or **brit milah**.

*****Peyos** is a Yiddish word for the long curls of hair that hang in front of the ears on ultra-Orthodox men and boys. Hasidic Jews wait until their sons are three years old before giving them their first haircut, at which time the hair is cut short but the *peyos* left long.

Ram Dass, spiritual leader and psychedelics enthusiast, was born Richard Alpert and bar mitzvahed in Newton, Mass. His father, George, was a founder of Brandeis University.

***Definition from the *Dictionary of Jewish Words*.
See **page xxv** for more information.

The First Haircut

By three, little boys have lots of hair.
They may look shaggy, like they just returned from an
    Outward Bound in *Azazel*
        or like Paul McCartney in the early days,
            when he'd shake his head and
        sweet-talk with his eyes from under those lashes
        or girly, especially with curls, like my friends'
            baby — Jewish — who they dressed in a
            Santa suit and brought to a holiday brunch.
By three, little boys are ready for a haircut.

It's the middle of the night on the 33rd day of counting
and the spring days are getting longer, minute
    upon minute.
It's warm enough to not wear your winter coat
and chilly enough that you can't wear sandals.
The bonfire blazes — as if for a coven, or s'mores on
    Memorial Day.

The rabbis do the barbering,
having taken lessons from the man who shares an
    office with the *mohel,*
and they chop-chop-chop-chop, lopping off excess,
leaving only *peyos* for the little boys to fiddle with
and a bad haircut to be remedied in the morning by a
    man with a red-and-white pole.
The hair slips through the rabbis' fingers like mercury
and is gathered to be kindling,
and thrown into the fire, which devours it.

Singed hair smells nasty, like a headline death,
not like little boys
who smell like mud and chocolate, and the sweet
     breath of their mothers.
So when the bonfire has eaten itself up
and the stink of ash has risen
little boys go to the barber.
Their fathers in black bring Hershey bars and
     dried apricots
and let their sons, who may be lonely for
     their thumbs,
burrow for as long as they want in their thick,
     black beards.

Ready to Receive (at Sinai)

To get ready to receive a gift,
to truly receive a gift,
a good gift,
let go of memories
of past gifts,
and of expectations,
or hopes
about what this new gift might be.
Let them go, free them like the firefly in your
    cupped hands.

Be open,
so open that you feel the wind enter, then leave,
    your body.
Be empty as your backyard's robin's nest in January.
Take off your shoes and stand;
feel your feet, grounding you, sand between your toes.
Breathe in your relationship with the gift-giver
and don't think about what you did
or did not do
to deserve a gift
this good gift,
this truly good gift.

To borrow from spiritual teacher Ram Dass:
Be Here Now
when you're there
in your Sinai,
your feet in the sand
not thinking about the gift
not remembering
not hoping or expecting

as the desert wind blows
and you breathe.

Stand there,
arms open,
eyes closed,
as ready as you can be
there
now
to receive
this gift,
this truly good gift.

SHAVUOT

Explanation of words, phrases, and concepts appearing in the Shavuot poems

SHAVUOT is an early-summer holiday, seven weeks after the first day of Passover and the exodus, which celebrates Moses's receiving the Ten Commandments at Mt. Sinai. It also celebrates the harvest of the first fruits of spring. In many congregations, people stay awake all night to study Torah. The Ten Commandments are read on the *Shavuot* morning service.

***A *blintz* is a folded pancake, like a crepe, typically filled with fruit or sweet cheese. It is traditional to eat blintzes on *Shavuot*.

For *Torah*/**Five Books of the Hebrew Bible,** see *Simchat Torah* explanations.

Kvell is to be pleased and take pride in another person's accomplishments, often of one's children.

God provided **manna** for the Jews to eat as they approached Mt. Sinai and waited for the Revelation. Exodus 16:31 — "The house of Israel named it manna; it was like coriander seed, white, and it tasted like wafers in honey."

****Yichud* is the short period of seclusion, immediately after a wedding ceremony, when the bride and groom are alone together for the first time as a married couple. Traditionally, couples who have fasted on their wedding day break the fast together during this time.

Zayde is the Yiddish word for grandfather.

***Definition from the *Dictionary of Jewish Words*. See **page xxv** for more information.

Fruit

We ate apples at the *seder*,
their flesh off-white, like day-old ice,
as if they'd never seen the sun,
all covered by a blanket of thick skin;
tough stuff, to keep the doctor away,
softened by wine and walnuts.

But now it's time for strawberries
the color of sunburn on a green-eyed girl,
heart-shaped, wearing green collars
that remind us where they came from,
and their own sweet smell, as intense as honeysuckle.
Another gift, summer, is just beyond the bend.

Books: The Giving of The Torah at Mt. Sinai

We have always loved books:

Hard covers like an embrace
holding between them pages of possibilities,
and words — squiggles of black on white —
which inspire, instruct,
intuit what we need or want.

They are rungs on a ladder, upward,
　　or rocks to pause on
　　on the ascent
　　up the mountain,
　　stories to grasp like a welcome stump
　　as the mist lifts
　　and the air gets thinner
　　and you can't look back or you'll fall.

We have always made room for books
from the beginning,
from that first time, to now.

Rules

Rules are not meant to inhibit you,
to trap you behind bars where you are,
straddling evil and good,
one foot stretching toward each side,
      but to reveal the extremes
      that most of us, even if we extended our arms
      as wide as the equator, wouldn't reach.

The rules that say "you shall not"
strip off humanity's holiday suit
to expose intent gone awry,
      the bleakest, blackest wrongs
      that can't be made right
      even by the fanciest footwork of lawyers
      or doctors who testify to insanity.

The rules that say "you shall"
are the bunch of perfect carrots — and you
   love carrots —
waiting for you on the farmer's porch just down
   the road,
which you'll never quite reach,
      but on the way there
      you fling pocketsful of corn to the chickens
      and pat the head of a brown-eyed cow
      and pour water for the day-laborers.

Manna

You've had manna many times:
At the end of a portage in Ontario,
        with loons and moose and rainy beaver dams,
In Manhattan, at intermission, in a masterpiece,
At recess, on the day you learned to tell time,
On a bike, at the top of a sweaty and determined hill,
During your first meal in a new home,
        when the air still smells like someone else
        and your dust hasn't yet taken its space,
In the air, over Denver, when you're in aluminum,
    suspended,
And in the *yichud* room, right after the glass has
    been smashed.

Its seeds stick in your teeth like memory,
        its crunch, like an apple just fallen from the tree,
And the honey reminds you of healing.
Manna, a chameleon, has always been here,
        its recipe written on a dusty cloud with shards
                of glass,
        over Denver, sung at just the right time, by loons.

Staying up All Night to Study

It's different from college
where you stoke up on coffee and sugar
(and stronger stuff for some)
to outsmart your circadian rhythms,
especially that darn lullaby,
the one that whispers to you –
and your laptop — to relax, and give in to sleep mode,
and put aside your books, and dream.

This all-nighter at synagogue
is all because of the gift of a book,
that Big Book with the unforgettable name,
with its no-mistakes-tolerated editing.

What they say is that on the morning
God was going to give the *Torah* to the Israelites
   — a hefty present, one to pass down
   like the silver and china and Lladro figurines —
they overslept and kept God waiting on the
  mountaintop.
    (And you don't keep God waiting in the morning,
    on a mountaintop,
    even if you bring an extra latte and a
      cranberry scone.)
So to repent, months before *Yom Kippur*,
we stay awake and study the Book all night.

The synagogue smells like wax, warm wood,
over-the-hill lilies of the valley,
and the slightly stale decaf in the synagogue kitchen.

Don't wear a watch. Give yourself to the ticking time
instead of trying to trick it
into submission.
As the night gets darker, then light,
dream of words with feathery wings,
flying over houses that breathe out and in with sleep.
Dream of books that flap their covers
to soar higher than any mountaintop
to meet the morning.
Dream of unwound parchment riding waves of air
like an enormous flying carpet,
hitch a bumpy ride and go with it where it goes
where it goes is good
morning.

My Mother's Blintzes

My mother's from-scratch *blintzes* were sweet,
soft, and mushy,
like her breasts
in her old-lady hugs.

The insides were loose,
runny sweet cheese
uncontained,
like the stories she told, and again,
often with different facts
so I don't know what is true.

The recipe is from the "Old Country,"
from her mother, and before,
like the inherited nose (that I have),
and wrinkled hands (that I don't have yet),
and shapeless fears (which I had.)

The *blintzes* were browned in butter on the outside,
and tucked close at the edges
so nothing leaked (like the family secrets.)

They were reserved for special occasions,
like the silver (stainless steel),
and the crystal (plain glass),
and embroidered linen (stained with decades of too-
  sweet wine.)

My mother's *blintzes* were difficult to make,
but because they were from the "Old Country"
— which she never saw, but somehow idealized —
she spent the time,

247

having learned how-much-of-this-and-that
from her mother.
Perhaps the how-to's came from my mother's
   own *bubbe* —
but none of that generation made it over.

I surprise myself:
Me, who treasures the two sweaters my *bubbe* knit for
   my Ginny doll,
and my grandfather's Yiddish prayer books, two
   coin banks,
and his address book
— my only tangible legacy —
I've never tried to make my mother's *blintzes*.
And it's not because she never wrote down the recipe.

I tell myself they're too much work,
and the frozen ones are fine.
But in truth, my mother *owned* those *blintzes*
— perfect from-scratch *blintzes* —
and certain things should die along with death.

In College They're Called "All-Nighters"

There's sweetness in the sunrise
that arrives when you're bone weary,
your bleary eyes saying "no more,"
when you've heard the clock tick beyond hours you
    usually don't see
and, if he still existed, a milkman would deliver to
    your door.

There's welcome in the dawn
that arrives when your brain has overcome your
    body's resistance,
your mind needing rest time now — no more —
when you've grappled with the Five Books you don't
    usually see.
And, if he still lived, your *Zayde* would walk you to
    your door.

There's release in the light of morning
that arrives when your heartsoul has inhaled
    and expanded,
when your stubbly friends can't conceal their fatigue,
    which you don't usually see.
And, if God still is, you would feel delivered
— an opening door —
maybe more.

Seven Weeks

So much can happen in seven weeks

A boy drops octaves
A baby sprouts wings in its wet womb world
And Venice becomes more than just a dream

A father dies, another diagnosed
A mother remarries a friend
And what started as seeds in the dank, dark depths
    reveals color and velvety smell

A sturdy house receives a new coat
The cats shed theirs
And a smudgy finger flips the calendar, twice

A friend moves miles
A woman climbs mountains
And a girl sheds her wobbly training wheels

A child transforms words into reading
A car gives out at last, like patience
And the people who've set out, unchained,
finally find their footing.

Since Exodus: Wandering Jews

It's been seven weeks since we left home,
seven weeks of wandering,
seven weeks of roaming, of setting up then
    tearing down,
seven weeks of not getting attached, and worse,
    getting unattached
like an ill-fated embryo,
seven weeks of wanting to put out sticky tentacles
    and implant,
Seven weeks of rootlessness,
Seven weeks of staying aboveground.

A healthy plant sends out roots.
They search down, deep, into the dark earth
whether it's mud, sand, chalk or dust.
Their urge is to mingle and expand,
to open and exhale,
and let in the brown, nutty underground food
to make a home, a network of veins.

It's been seven weeks since we left home,
Seven weeks of wandering,
Seven weeks of roaming, of setting up then
    tearing down,
Seven weeks of not getting attached, and worse,
    getting unattached
like an ill-fated embryo,

But seven weeks of persevering,
Seven weeks of one foot in front of the other
Seven weeks of moving forward.

TISHA B'AV

Explanation of words, phrases, and concepts appearing in the Tisha b'Av poems

***TISHA B'AV is a minor holiday, marking the dates of the destruction of both ancient holy Temples in Jerusalem. Because it's a mourning holiday, *Tisha b'Av* observances include fasting for 24 hours and not engaging in pleasurable activities. It falls during late July or early August.

Even though Jews don't believe in a Messiah who will appear in human shape, it is believed that *Tisha b'Av* will be the day on which the Messiah will be born.

***Definition from the *Dictionary of Jewish Words*.
See **page xxv** for more information.

Menu

on the night before *Tisha b'Av*
we're supposed to eat a meal of mourning
including lentils, or hard-cooked eggs,
and raw vegetables and fruit.
    But that's how I've learned to eat all the time
    to take care of my heart
    to prevent stagnation
    to keep crisp and simple.

on the night before *Tisha b'Av*
we're supposed to eat a meal of mourning
including bread dipped in ashes.
    But I've burned my bagel many times
    and I don't mind the taste of buttered after-fire;
    also, I've downed marshmallows that have fallen
        in the grill
    and I'll eat the shell of blackness that collapsed
        in on the white.

Still, the doing-without of this particular meal,
on this particular night,
somehow prepares me to mourn our losses,
the doing-without of our home.

Laying a Foundation

We understand.
Twice, the Holy Temple
was burned to the ground.
Twice, the believers
had to sift through rubble, char, and ash.
Twice, the people
had only crumbs to feed the Phoenix.
Twice, we had to say yes, in spite of, to keep our faith,
   in the face of.

And draped in sackcloth and ashes, we learned
that religion isn't baked in bricks,
or slathered in mortar.

In the two years between January, 1995, and January 1997, at
least 67 Black churches in the South were destroyed by fire,
most of a suspicious nature.

Tisha b'Av at Schroon River Cottages

This is one of those holy days I never observed
didn't know about
hadn't learned about.
It was the middle of summer, for God's sake,
and we were in the Adirondacks.
Our rabbi was vacationing somewhere
and the rest of the congregation was scattered, like ash
or sand or bits of sycamore bark.

It was one of those holidays I knew was built
around the destruction of the Temple,
and we were supposed to fast.
But what with fleshy purple blueberries in
    Fiestaware bowls
and people inviting us for pancakes
or fish fries from the bounty of Schroon River,
during these drowsy days so full of nothing we just
    didn't want to do without.

And it wasn't one of the Big Ones, like a High Holy Day,
a holiday we had to do
because everyone else did, even if not so much.
It landed, rudely, on a hot day,
when the melted-butter-yellow sunshine
chased everyone into the river.

Decades later,
after I'd learned about *Tisha b'Av*,
I visited the Adirondacks in August
and found that Schroon River Cottages had
    been destroyed.

I understood, and I wept

Weeping

Weeping is deeper than crying.
It happens when a soul contracts,
squeezing life-liquid out like a sponge too tired to
   hold it in.

Weeping is saltier than sobbing.
It's what's left when a spirit decomposes
and frees what's essential to escape.

Weeping is more profound than shedding tears.
It's what happens when a person dissolves
and doesn't just express pain, but becomes it.

To Welcome the Messiah

If all the women gathered in the congregation
decide to spritz themselves
with perfume
to welcome the Messiah (who, they don't know,
may be allergic),
they'd better have decided,
in advance,
and reached consensus,
on Passion,
or Obsession,
or Tabu,
or else there'll be such a stink —
worse than New Jersey, or the smell of
   burning rubber —
that the Messiah, nauseated, will walk away.

Tisha b'Av is sometimes regarded as the birthday of the
Messiah, so "In some Sephardic and Eastern communities,
women put on perfume to welcome King Messiah." (Arthur
Waskow, *Seasons of Our Joy*.)

Birthday Questions for the Messiah

Should I sing to you, or do you prefer a low-key
celebration? Would you be embarrassed if I threw a
surprise party for you in a restaurant?

You want a cake, don't you? Will you scrape the
buttercream frosting to the side of your plate, or will
you claim the extra flowers? Do you have enough
strength to blow out your candles?

Have you received a lot of cards? Did people get your
address right? How many cards came online?

Do you expect calls from family and friends who
live far away? Are you all on the same phone
plan, so you can contact each other regularly and
inexpensively?

How do you feel about getting older? Do you lie about
your age?

Do you discourage people from giving you gifts but
really like receiving them? Do you save wrapping
paper to reuse?

    And,
    how in the world, this world,
        are you going to save us?

TU B'AV

Explanation of words, phrases, and concepts appearing in the Tu b'Av poems

TU B'AV — one week after *Tisha b'Av*, the saddest day in the Jewish calendar — served as a matchmaking day for unmarried women in the Second Temple period. It was almost unnoticed in the Jewish calendar for many centuries but has been rejuvenated in recent decades, especially in Israel, as a sort of Valentine's Day.

The festival of *Tu b'Av* (the fifteenth of Av) is called "the happiest day in the Jewish year" in the *Mishnah* (*Ta'anit*, Chapter 4). "The practice on this day was for single Israelite women to go out in the vineyards, dressed in white, and dance before the young men. Coupling ensued." *Jewniverse*

Dancing in Vineyards/Looking for You

Before Tom gave you my number
     You, with the beard and bald, looking rabbinic,
        my favorite type,
     Me, with untouched grey hair and an
          unconventional appearance by choice,
I danced in a lot of vineyards.

I repeat: A lot of vineyards.

I had an outfit I wore each time,
a cross between Princess Leia
and Marilyn Monroe's white halter from *The Seven
   Year Itch*
     with its penchant for flying high in an updraft.
Over the years, it stained light purple in spots,
     mostly near the hem
     which happens when you romp around
        in vineyards.

I went barefoot,
wanting to feel my feet on the ground.
And I went stag,
most of my girlfriends, by then,
having coupled.

It's difficult to figure out what dance to dance
     to express who you are
     and who you're hoping to attract
when you're dancing without a partner.

Do you present yourself as complete, your dance a
    whole, alone,
        or is your dance one of lacking:
        The Fox without the Trot?

You, my darling, didn't seem to mind
that my dress was stained from years of
    vineyard dancing,
or that I seemed okay, not sweaty with desperation,
dancing my dance alone:
        A Lindy without the Hop,
        the Electric without the Slide.

Late in the evening
you jumped up and joined me:
        You were a Cha to match my Cha.
        The Conga to my Line,
        the Hully to my Gully,
and all these years later, you still are.

How lucky that Tom gave you my number!

About the Author

photo SKIP ATKINS

Janet Ruth Falon is an award-winning poet and journalist, and a writing teacher. A former newspaper reporter and magazine editor, she is author of *The Jewish Journaling Book* and two books about gender respect. She has also written for the The *New York Times*, *The Philadelphia Zoo*, *WHYY television*, and more.

Janet has taught a variety of writing classes at The University of Pennsylvania, Temple University, Gratz College, synagogues, churches, and art museums, and teaches expressive writing and journaling to people with cancer. She also works with people on an individual basis.

She lives in Elkins Park, Pennsylvania, with her husband Cary Mazer, daughter Hope Falon-Mazer, and their two cats, Mendel and Rifka.

Made in the USA
Middletown, DE
13 April 2021

37497065R00175